The HERITAGE BOOK

1999

Edna McCann

Prentice Hall Canada Inc.
Scarborough, Ontario

Prentice-Hall, Inc., Upper Saddle River, New Jersey
Prentice-Hall International (UK) Limited, London
Prentice-Hall of Australia, Pty. Limited, Sydney
Prentice-Hall Hispanoamericana, S.A., Mexico City
Prentice-Hall of India Private Limited, New Delhi
Prentice-Hall of Japan, Inc., Tokyo
Simon & Schuster Southeast Asia Private Limited, Singapore
Editora Prentice-Hall do Brasil, Ltda., Rio de Janeiro

ISBN 0-13-982877-X

Director of Trade Publishing: Robert Harris
Copy Editors: Linda Cahill, Kelli Howey
Production Coordinator: Shannon Potts
Art Director: Mary Opper
Cover Design: Julia Hall
Cover Image: Charlene Daley
Page Layout: B. J. Weckerle

1 2 3 4 5   F 02 01 00 99 98

Printed and bound in Canada

Literary Credits
Page 68 "She Always Leaned to Watch for Us" by Margaret Widdemer is reprinted
with permission of John D. Widdemer.
Page 126 "Harvest of the Years" by Grace Noll Crowell from Bright Harvest ©
HarperCollins.

Photo Credits
Winter
Gord Handley, Gord Handley, Gord Handley, Nikki Abraham, Florence Gillespie,
Charlene Daley, Nikki Abraham, Vince Farr
Spring
Gord Handley, Nikki Abraham, Gord Handley, Nikki Abraham, Florence Gillespie,
Florence Gillespie, Gord Handley, Florence Gillespie
Summer
Charlene Daley, Florence Gillespie, Gord Handley, Gord Handley, Gord Handley,
Charlene Daley, Gord Handley, Gord Handley
Fall
Nikki Abraham, Gord Handley, Gord Handley, Gord Handley, Charlene Daley, Gord
Handley, Gord Handley, Gord Handley

Visit the Prentice Hall Canada Web site! Send us your comments, browse our catalogues, and more. **www.phcanada.com**

Introduction

When I began to put together this year's *Heritage Book*, it struck me anew how life never ceases to provide inspiration. Our bounty of experiences teaches us to grow, to learn, to appreciate, to give and to love. From the earth-shaking, pivotal events of our lives to the small occurrences of the everyday, each moment is something to cherish.

As the years pass I have come to realize that one of the secrets of happiness is to cultivate a love for the "little" things: the flash of a smile, hot tea on a cold afternoon, a soothing voice, the way a summer evening slowly deepens into night.

I hope that this *Heritage Book* will bring you treasures that you can call your own, and that you can share with those around you.

Edna McCann

January

Friday January 1

FACING the New Year, we pledge ourselves to follow through the coming year the light which God gave us: the light of Truth, wherever it may lead; the light of Freedom, revealing new opportunities for individual development and social service; the light of Faith, opening new visions of the better world to be; the light of Love, daily binding brother to brother and man to God in ever closer bonds of friendship and affection.

Guided by this light, we shall go forward to the work of another year with steadfastness and confidence.

A new year is a gracious gift. It is a time to look back at our accomplishments and look forward to dreams and hopes for the coming year. In this last year before the new millennium, I wish for all of us peace, joy and happiness.

Saturday January 2

TO comprehend a man's life, it is necessary to know not merely what he does, but also what he purposely leaves undone. There is a limit to the work that can be gotten out of a human body or a human brain, and he is a wise man who wastes no energy on pursuits for which he is not fitted; and he is still wiser who, from among the things that he can do well, chooses and resolutely follows the best.

W. E. Gladstone

Sunday January 3

BUT now, O Lord, thou art our father; we are the clay, and thou our potter; and we all are the work of thy hand.

Be not wroth very sore, O Lord, neither remember iniquity for ever: behold, see, we beseech thee, we are all thy people.

Isaiah 64:8–9

Monday January 4

WHERE your pleasure is, there is your treasure. Where your treasure is, there is your heart. Where your heart is, there is your happiness.

St. Augustine

Tuesday January 5

Each new year I seem to need a longer period to recover from the unsettled routines of the holiday season.

This year, in particular, was exceptionally tiring. For the first time in nearly a decade, our entire family was together for Christmas dinner.

It was a wonderful occasion, with many cries of, "My, you haven't changed a bit," and, "I am so happy to see you—it has been so long!" There was much hustle and bustle as we caught up, all the while putting the last-minute touches on the dinner preparations.

When needed a break, I took my leave quietly and retreated to the peace of my little "apartment" in my daughter's home. I was just sitting down with a cup of tea when there came a quiet rap on my closed door. I was surprised to see my sister, Sarah, her husband, Richard, my brother, Ben, and his wife, Marie, smiling rather sheepishly. "Edna, if we promise to be very quiet, may we join you for a rest?" I laughed and said yes immediately. We old folks need to stick together.

Wednesday January 6

THIS is Epiphany, the day that the Western Church commemorates the coming of the Three Wise Men to Bethlehem.

In Quebec, on the eve of Epiphany, there is a Twelfth Night celebration. Following a tradition that dates back to the middle ages in France, French Canadian families make a special cake called the *Galette des Rois*. This cake contains a bean, and whoever finds the bean becomes the "king" or "queen" of the party. The person who has been given this honour is then responsible for choosing and organizing the activities for the evening.

It is an enjoyable night before the more serious religious time of the Epiphany.

Thursday January 7

I DON'T think that we ever stop being mothers. Helen, a neighbour, was driving me to the grocery store during a winter storm. As we came up to a corner, a policeman was directing traffic. Helen rolled down her window and shouted, "Young man, put on your scarf! It's much too cold to be out here without it." The young officer smiled and continued to direct the oncoming cars, but Helen persisted. "What would your mother say?" she hollered. Finally, with a laugh, the policeman hurried to his cruiser, took out a scarf and wrapped it around his neck.

Helen smiled, waved, rolled up her window, and with a satisfied "There!" we continued on our way.

Friday January 15

TODAY is the birthdate of Dr. Martin Luther King Jr., the great African-American civil rights leader. In his honour, I offer the poem "Brotherhood," by Grace Noll Crowell.

BROTHERHOOD...one simple singing word:
A word that pictures mankind linked with God.
We say it over and our hearts are stirred,
We view the pathway that our feet have trod,
And we know we somehow missed the way, when men
Have fought their mad wars, time and time again.

A brotherhood of nations...every land
Freed from dark suspicion, doubt and greed,
Opening their doors with fearless hand
To meet a neighbouring people's desperate need.
How beautiful it is to contemplate!
Let us work for it before it is too late.

The brotherhood of man...oh, strive for it,
That wars and their wild rumors all may cease.
It will be as if a lighted torch were lit,
And a bewildered world at last will find its peace.
All this will be if mankind only would
Unite in universal brotherhood.

Friday January 8

IT is good to be rich, and to be strong, but it is a better thing to be beloved of many friends.

Euripides

Saturday January 9

THE whole wide world is silver,
With diamonds here and there;
On a snow-filled winter morning,
There's beauty everywhere.

The air is crisp and bracing,
The treetops dressed in lace;
You walk in breathless silence,
And wonder lights your face.

The sparrow tracks are myriad,
A red squirrel scampers by,
And from the cedar woodlot,
You hear a blue jay cry.

There's magic all around you,
At any time of year,
You only need awareness,
To see and feel and hear.

My thanks to the unknown author for these words of winter's beauty.

Saturday January 16

I DON'T expect anyone to fully appreciate that a mother makes more decisions in one morning than the Supreme Court makes in three years.

Erma Bombeck

Sunday January 17

A ND Jesus said unto them, I am the bread of life: he that cometh to me shall never hunger; and he that believeth in me, shall never thirst.

John 6:35

Monday January 18

T HE beauty of a soul shines out when a man bears with composure one heavy mischance after another, not because he does not feel them, but because he is a man of high and heroic temper.

Aristotle

Tuesday January 19

M Y dear friend, Jake Frampton, came by for dinner this evening. Jake regularly spoils me by bringing me books, old and new, that he knows I will enjoy. This evening was no exception.

Jake brought a number of books, but the ones I'm most looking forward to reading are an illustrated *Travel Guide to New Zealand*, and Frommer's *Guide to New Zealand*. You see, my daughter Julia works for a multinational corporation, and she will be going to New Zealand later this month, or in early February. Her sisters Marg, Mary and I love to hear about the trips that Julia takes, but we always enjoy her stories much more when we are familiar with the area that she is visiting.

New Zealand is a country that I am very interested in, as I have, on several occasions, seen documentary films that have shown the extraordinary beauty of the small land "down under."

I feel very blessed to have a friend who is so generous and thoughtful, and I will enjoy the books all the more knowing that they were given to me by a true friend.

Wednesday January 20

THIS recipe for acorn squash soup is rich tasting but surprisingly low in calories—only 92 per serving. Add a salad and warm biscuits and you have an easy but satisfying meal.

Acorn Squash Soup

2 tbsp. butter or margarine
1 red or green pepper, chopped
1 small onion, chopped
1 tbsp. minced fresh ginger
1 clove garlic, minced
2 medium acorn squash (about 2 lb.)
2 3/4 cups chicken broth
1 tsp. dried thyme
1 tsp. salt
1/4 tsp. black pepper
1/2 cup half and half cream
chopped fresh parsley for garnish (optional)

In a large pot, melt butter over low heat. Add pepper, onion, ginger, garlic, and cook until the onion is softened, about 8 minutes. Meanwhile, peel, seed and cube the squash, then add it to the pot with broth, thyme, salt and pepper.

Increase the heat to high, cover and bring to a boil. Reduce the heat to low and continue to cook until the squash is very tender, about 30 minutes. Remove from the heat and stir in the half and half. Purée in batches until smooth. Return to the pot over low heat; cook until heated through, 2–3 minutes. Transfer to a serving bowl and garnish with parsley if desired. Makes 8 servings.

Thursday January 21

OCCASIONALLY, I am lucky enough to receive notes from readers as far away as England, Ireland and even Australia. Often I am given letters or cards of thanks from readers who have enjoyed *The Heritage Book* for many years.

I am extremely flattered that anyone would take the time to write to me, and many of these letters have moved me to tears.

Although time prohibits me from answering many of these communications, I do appreciate them immensely. I would like to mention a card that I received from Bonnie Uhryn, the activity director at Trent Valley Lodge, a nursing home in Trenton, Ontario.

In her letter Bonnie explained, "For a number of years, I have included the daily readings from *The Heritage Book* in my morning program. By sharing this wonderful book with so many, you have indeed become a part of our lives, and a cherished friend.... You have touched so many with your kind words, devotions, poems, personal and family adventures. We thank you from the bottom of our hearts for sharing all this with us."

It is I who now thank Bonnie for her kind words. A letter such as this lifts my spirits as almost nothing else can. Thank you, Bonnie, and my friends at the Trent Valley Lodge.

Friday January 22

ICAN'T imagine a home without laughter, a world so devoid of humour that there's never a chuckle or laugh. The laughter in our home is its heartbeat. It's the fuel for the warmth we share and the switch for the light we shine. Laughter leads us, kneads us and sometimes, helps bleed us of torments and woes.

R. Talbert

Saturday January 23

IF a man walks in the woods for love of them half of each day, he is in danger of being regarded as a loafer. But if he spends his day as a speculator, shearing off those woods and making the earth bald before her time, he is esteemed an industrious and enterprising citizen.

Henry David Thoreau

Sunday January 24

TRULY my soul waiteth upon God; from him cometh my salvation. He only is my rock and my salvation; he is my defence; I shall not be greatly moved.

Psalm 62

Monday January 25

THIS is the date that, all across the country, people of Scottish descent and their friends will gather to honour that wonderful Scottish poet Robert Burns.

Flow gently, sweet Afton, among thy green braes!
Flow gently, I'll sing thee a song in thy praise!
My Mary's asleep by the murmuring stream—
Flow gently, sweet Afton, disturb not her dream!

Tuesday January 26

MY good friends Will and Muriel stopped in to visit today. While we enjoyed a cup of tea, we discussed a favourite topic—the Canadian winter. Will had a number of suggestions that will help us avoid illness or injury at this time of year, which is particularly hazardous for us seniors.

Drink plenty of water. When homes are dried out by the heat, it is easy to become dehydrated.

Have an expert check your furnace for carbon monoxide leaks, which can be fatal. There are alarms now that can detect the deadly gas.

Don't shovel snow if you are not in good shape. You could hurt yourself—or even worse, you could end up having a heart attack.

Wash your hands frequently. This gets rid of the cold and flu germs that you pick up by shaking hands with people or touching surfaces that may have germs. As well, seniors are advised to get a flu shot before the season is upon us.

If you should become ill, remember to get lots of rest, drink lots of liquids and have chicken noodle soup—it's a miracle cure for all ills (your mother told you!).

Wednesday January 27

MY daughter Julia has come to me with an extraordinary proposal. As I mentioned, she is going to New Zealand—and she would like me to accompany her. Some of her trip will, of course, be spent doing business in several of the larger cities, but she plans to take several weeks to sightsee on both islands. I am so overwhelmed by her offer that I hardly know what to say. Part of me wants to rush up and pack my bags immediately, but then I think to myself, "Edna, for gracious sake, you are far too old to be jaunting off to the other side of the world."

Thursday January 28

TRAVEL, in the younger sort, is part of education; in the elder, a part of experience.

Francis Bacon

Friday January 29

IT'S only in the country that we grow to
  understand
The meaning and the mystery of nature's
  wonderland…
And when we walk the tinselled track along the
  woodland way,
We come to love the cold clear beauty of a
  winter's day.

Saturday January 30

AFTER many hours of deliberation, I have
made my decision. I am going to New
Zealand with Julia. I remembered my husband
George's advice: "Life is short and very fragile.
Do what makes you happy."

We will be leaving a week from today, so I will
be very busy between now and then. I can hardly
believe this is happening to me, but I know that
I am going to enjoy every single moment!

Sunday January 31

IF I take the wings of the morning and dwell
in the uttermost parts of the sea; even there
shall Thy hand lead me, and Thy right hand shall
hold me.

Psalms 133:9–10

February

Monday February 1

I watched a lonely sparrow
As winds with violence blew,
Moving slowly with ruffled feathers,
Its feet were cold I knew.
Snow lay deep upon the ground,
There was no food to see;
Without a doubt a little bird
Was hungry as can be.

Beneath a tree was a spot
Where the ground was bare,
And no sparrow could be seen
As I sprinkled breadcrumbs there.
Soon as I was out of sight,
I heard a chirping sound,
And when the sparrows had their fill
No crumbs were on the ground.

One lonely sparrow spread the news
That food was to be had—
It only took a slice of bread,
To make the sparrows glad.
While the winter snowflakes fall,
For you, I write these words,
Asking that you not forget
To feed the little birds.

THIS poem, "Winter's Birds," is a reminder of how much these tiny creatures need our help. My thanks to the unknown author.

Tuesday February 2

TODAY, Canadians wait anxiously to hear the weather report of "Wiarton Willie," the groundhog who predicts our weather for the rest of winter.

I had to laugh at my friend, Mary McConnell. Several years ago, Mary called me on Groundhog Day.

"I want you to know, Edna, that we won't be seeing six more weeks of winter. If that groundhog even attempts to come out of his hole, I am going to choke him!"

I wasn't altogether sure that she was joking!

Wednesday February 3

THERE is a particular beauty about godly old age—the beauty of holiness. Husband and wife who have fought the world side by side, who have made common stock of joy or sorrow, and become aged together, are not infrequently found curiously alike in personal appearance, in pitch and tone of voice, just as twin pebbles on the beach, exposed to the same tidal influences, are each other's alter ego.

A. Smith

Thursday February 4

JUST about a year ago, we were treated to two weeks of athletic competition from the Winter Olympic Games of Nagano, Japan. Canadian athletes had their share of both incredible medal wins and disappointing losses, and it was a joy to watch these young people representing our country. What impressed me most was the sportsmanship and camaraderie displayed by the athletes of every country.

Who couldn't be moved by the sight of the gold-medal-winning cross-country skier, who waited in falling snow at the finish line to congratulate the last-place finisher on completing his first Olympic race! To me, this is what the Olympics are all about.

Friday February 5

TOMORROW is the big day—the day we leave on our incredible journey to New Zealand. I have been pinching myself to be sure that this is really happening to me.

I was agonizing over my packing, not wanting to take too much (or too little), but I think I am finally ready to go. This evening, Marg and Bruce had a small "bon voyage" dinner, and my grandchildren presented me with a beautiful new camera for the trip. I am looking forward to recording every wonderful moment.

Photography records the gamut of feelings written on the human face—the beauty of the earth and skies that man has inherited; and the wealth and confusion man has created. It is a major force in explaining man to man.

Edward Steichen

The virtue of the camera is not the power it has to transform the photographer into an artist, but the impulse it gives him to keep on looking.

Brooks Atkinson

Life is not about significant details, illuminated in a flash, fixed forever. Photographs are.

Susan Sontag

Saturday February 6

Julia is sound asleep in the seat beside me, but I can't seem to nod off. We are in the air, somewhere between Los Angeles and Auckland. We've had a delicious meal, the movie has ended, and the lights are dimmed, but my mind is still racing.

Do I have everything? Where did I put my passport? Will I be strong enough to truly enjoy this trip?

All of these thoughts keep me from resting, so I will do what I always do when I am unable to sleep.

"Dear Lord, here I am on one of the most incredible journeys of my life, and I am not truly sure that I should be here, but, since I am, I ask that you be with me and help me to enjoy this trip to the very best of my ability."

The flight attendant has brought me an extra pillow and blanket. I believe that I am ready for sleep.

Sunday February 7

O GOD, our heavenly father, who art present in thy power in every place: preserve, we beseech thee, all who travel by land, by water or by air; surround them with thy loving care; protect them from every danger; and bring them in safety to their journey's end.

Monday February 8

HOW do I describe my first view of New Zealand? Beautiful, resplendent, magnificent—even these superlatives seem inadequate to try to paint the picture of the deep blue-green water, the wild flowers that are blooming everywhere, and the sun shining on the hundreds of billowing sails as the yachts skim across the waters of Auckland's harbour.

We landed very early in the morning, and the limousine ride into downtown Auckland seemed to pass very quickly. Julia and I were like young schoolgirls as we pointed out the sights to one another.

The downtown area is a wonderful blend of high-rise buildings, busy boutiques, and chic outdoor cafés. According to our driver, the downtown and harbour areas are being made even more beautiful as the city prepares for the America's Cup yacht race, to be held later this year.

Our hotel is luxurious beyond my wildest dreams, and the view is extraordinary. From our window, I can see the Harbour Bridge over the waters of Waitemata Harbour. As well, I can see Rangitoto Island, the result of a volcanic eruption only 700 or so years ago.

Although I have been standing here for more than an hour, I can't bear to pull myself away for fear that somehow it will all disappear.

Tuesday February 9

Let fate do her worst, there are relics of joy,
Bright dreams of the past, which she cannot
     destroy;
Which come in the night-time of sorrow and care,
And bring back the features that joy used to wear,
Long, long be my heart with such memories fill'd!

Like the vase, in which roses have once been
    distill'd—
You may break, you may shatter the vase, if you
    will,
But the scent of the roses will hang round it still.

Thomas Moore

Wednesday February 10

TO improve the golden moment of opportunity and catch the good that is within our reach, is the great art of life.

Samuel Johnson

Thursday February 11

GOD'S best gift to us is not things but opportunities.

Alice W. Rollins

Friday February 12

Early in the morning, I walked down to the harbour, where I enjoyed a cup of tea at an outdoor café. The café had a view of the Fuller's Ferry dock, and I was able to see the ferries as they came and went to the many islands just inside and outside of the harbour.

I asked the young lady who was my waitress which of the cruises she would recommend.

"Well now, let's find out, shall we?" she said in her lovely Kiwi accent.

"Which cruise would you take if you were a visitor?" she asked in a loud voice to the other patrons.

Before I knew it there were about seven or eight people pulling chairs up to my table.

"Where are you from?" "What have you seen?" "Don't miss One Tree Hill" and so on.

I decided to start with the Harbour Explorer Cruise, which allowed me to get off and explore Devonport, where the Maori say their great ancestral canoe, *Tainui*, first touched land in this area. I saw a bronze sculpture topped by a Korotangi (weeping dove), one of the birds that the Maori brought with them from their homeland, that is a memorial to the event. I wandered past the Esplanade Hotel and in and out of the many shops along Victoria Road. I was a tired but happy tourist when I returned to our hotel that evening.

Saturday February 13

IF a man does not make new acquaintances as he advances through life, he will soon find himself alone. A man, sir, must keep his friendship in constant repair.

Samuel Johnson

Sunday February 14

FOR this Valentine's Day, I have chosen the beautiful words of the 13th chapter of Corinthians:

LOVE is patient, love is kind, and is not jealous: love does not act unbecomingly; it does not seek its own, is not provoked, does not take into account a wrong suffered, does not rejoice in unrighteousness, but rejoices with the truth; bears all things, believes all things, hopes all things, endures all things.

Love never fails.

But now abide faith, hope, love. These three; but the greatest of these is love.

Monday February 15

WHATU ngarongaro he yangata toitu he whenua
"Man perishes but the land remains."

Maori proverb

Tuesday February 16

JULIA and I have been visiting the northernmost part of the North Island, Cape Reinga, where the Tasman Sea meets the Pacific Ocean. We were able to see the waves, nearly ten metres high, crashing over the Columbus Reef. As the tour bus thundered along the hard-packed sands of Ninety-Mile Beach, our driver's informative commentary made it easy to imagine a time, not so long ago, when the first explorers arrived to explore the varied landscape that is New Zealand.

En route to Cape Reinga, we stopped at the *mangamuka marae* (meeting place) to share a remarkable Maori cultural experience. The Maori guide explained the function of the *marae* and gave us much insight into their heritage, traditions and modern-day lives.

From there, we returned to Paihia, in the Bay of Islands. On the advice of our tour guide, we took a ten-minute ferry ride to Russell, which, in 1840, was the largest European settlement in the country. Julia and I chose to stay at the Duke of Marlborough Hotel, New Zealand's very first hotel. The rooms have old-world charm, there is a beautiful dining room, and the covered veranda is a gathering place for guests and locals alike. It is a perfect place to enjoy this happy blend of history and natural beauty.

Wednesday February 17

THIS morning, Julia and I attended a service for Ash Wednesday in Christ Church, the oldest surviving church in New Zealand. Inside the church, which dates back to 1836, we sat on needlepoint pew cushions crafted by local residents. This little church, in Russell, was an exquisite place to hear the collect for today.

Almighty and everlasting God, who hatest nothing that thou hast made, and dost forgive the sins of all them that are penitent: create and make in us new and contrite hearts, that we worthily lamenting our sins, and acknowledging our wretchedness, may obtain of thee, the God of all mercy, perfect remission and forgiveness; through Jesus Christ our Lord, Amen.

Thursday February 18

IF the day and the night are such that you greet them with joy, and life emits a fragrance like flowers and sweet-scented herbs, is more elastic, more starry, more immortal—that is your success.

Henry David Thoreau

Friday February 19

THE days that make us happy make us wise.

John Masefield

Saturday February 20

JULIA and I are now in "wonderful, windy Wellington. "On our 11-hour train journey from Auckland, we passed through the gamut of scenic beauty that is New Zealand: snow-covered mountains, three active volcanoes, valleys densely clothed in green rain forests, rivers raging through deep gorges and then flowing peacefully between gentle hills, herds of cattle and flocks of sheep grazing on the green grass of the rolling farmlands, sweeps of sandy beaches and rocky headlands washed by sea waves.

Wellington, New Zealand's cultural centre, has a magnificent harbour and a lovely blend of narrow streets, Edwardian buildings and modern highrises of concrete and glass. The hills surrounding the city core are dotted with homes, all of which seem to have a view of the city and the harbour.

Julia and I have enjoyed much of what Wellington has to offer—the World Dragon Boat Festival, the Kelburn Cable Car leading up to the Botanical Gardens, and the newest attraction, the "Te Papa" Museum, opened just one year ago.

The Te Papa Tongarewa, the Maori name for "Repository of Things Precious," is the country's first bicultural museum, and the magnificent five-storey building contains the Maori and *Pakeha* (Caucasian) history side by side. It is truly breathtaking.

Sunday February 21

FOR the whole world before thee is a little grain of the balance, yea as a drop of the morning dew that falleth down upon the earth. But Thou hast mercy upon all. For Thou lovest all things that are.

Wisdom of Solomon 11:22–24, The Apocrypha

Monday February 22

WE are all travellers in the wilderness of this world, and the best that we find in our travels is an honest friend.

Robert Louis Stevenson

One of the most exciting parts of this incredible journey has been the wonderful people that we have met. When we leave for home, many of my fondest memories will be not of what we saw, but of whom we met.

Tuesday February 23

TODAY, we had a most moving experience—but it almost didn't happen. Julia and I had lined up to visit the Parliament Buildings, only to be told that the 1:00 tour was full. We decided to stay in the area anyway.

Just a few blocks away was Old St. Paul's Church, recommended as a "must see" on our sightseeing itinerary. Built in 1865, using native timbers of *kauri, matai, totara* and *rimu*, the softly lit church, with its brilliant stained-glass windows, exudes a sense of warmth and serenity. Julia and I sat down to take in the beauty of the stained glass, when we heard the melodic strains of "Ave Maria," and a young man stepped to the pulpit and began to sing this glorious work. After just a few bars, a voice called from the back of the church, "The volume is good, Jack."

"Oh, please don't stop now," I heard myself saying.

"I'm practising for my sister's wedding on Saturday," he explained.

He began again and this time he sang "Ave Maria" in a voice that completely filled the church. When he had finished, I found that I had tears running down my cheeks. If not for a delay in our tour, we would have missed this very special treat.

Wednesday February 24

IF your name is to live at all, it is so much more to have it live in people's hearts rather than only in their brains. I don't know that one's eyes fill with tears when he thinks of the famous inventor of logarithms.

Oliver Wendell Holmes

Thursday February 25

IF you give me something I need more than you do, you've given me a gift. If you give me something you need more than I do, you've gifted me with love.

Merry Browne

Friday February 26

PLEASANT words are as a honeycomb, sweet to the soul, and health to the bones.

Saturday February 27

JULIA and I are enjoying our last day in New Zealand here in Christchurch, a city that feels quite English. In fact, the city centre is situated around the Christchurch Cathedral, and you could choose to go punting on the River Avon. Cricket is played in the many parks of the area.

A trip up Mount Cavendish in the gondola gave us a spectacular view of Christchurch and the Banks Peninsula.

It hardly seems possible that we have spent three weeks in this exquisite country. I am so pleased that I have taken a multitude of pictures—I don't know how else I would be able to remember all that we have seen or to share my memories with family members at home.

I am thankful that I made the decision to accompany Julia on this fabulous trip. I wouldn't have missed it for the world!

Sunday February 28

TEACH me to do Thy will; for Thou art my God: Thy spirit is good; lead me into the land of uprightness.

Psalms 148:10

March

Monday March 1

The best part of vacation
Though far and wide we roam,
Is when it's time to travel back
The trail that leads to home.
Strange roads and ways are thrilling
And mighty fine to see,
But when vacation's over
At home we long to be.

It's fine to see the wonders
And beauties of the land—
The mighty snow-capped mountains,
The rolling sea, the sand,
The city's man-made glory;
But when tired we have grown,
We turn our faces toward
The path that leads to home.

It's fine to see the northland,
The beauty of the west,
The south, the east, all so fair;
But somehow I love best
Of all the towns and cities,
Though far and wide we roam,
That little rambling village
At trail's end we call…home!

Tuesday March 2

THIS morning I feel as if I could sleep for a week. My body isn't quite sure if it is yesterday or tomorrow. We crossed the international date line, but I truly forget whether we moved back or ahead on that date. I'm sure that it will take me a bit of time to get over the "jet lag," but no matter how long it takes, every minute that I am resting will give me time to remember the wonderful weeks just past.

Wednesday March 3

MY son-in-law, John, made me laugh today with this story. In a discussion group at church, a number of seniors were speaking of formal and informal prayer.

One of the elderly men remarked, "You know, I do some of my best praying while I am driving my car."

His wife remarked in a quiet voice, "I do my best praying when you are driving too, dear."

Thursday March 4

THESE words from Elizabeth Coatsworth are from her work, "Personal Geography." This is but a brief portion, but it is well worth reading in its entirety.

"Outwardly I am an octogenarian, but inwardly I am every age, with the emotions and experience of each period. The important thing is that at each age I am myself. During much of my life, I was anxious to be what someone else wanted me to be. Now I have given up that struggle. I am what I am."

Friday March 5

ACCORDING to my sister-in-law, Marie, seed catalogues should be labelled "literature." All winter long my brother, Ben, sits in a comfortable chair by the fire and studies these books, as many would study the classics.

"When Ben looks at these catalogues, he doesn't just see advertisements for various types of flowers, he actually envisions his whole garden, as it will look in July and August. A book that makes you dream must be great literature, don't you think?"

Saturday March 6

BOOKS are the food of youth, the delight of old age; the ornament of prosperity, the refuge and comfort of adversity; a delight at home, and no hindrance abroad; companions in the night, in travelling, in the country.

Marcus Tullius Cicero

Sunday March 7

BE ye therefore followers of God, as dear children; and walk in love, as Christ hath also loved us, and hath given himself for us, an offering and a sacrifice to God for a sweet-smelling saviour.

Ephesians 5:1

Monday March 8

SUCCESSFUL living requires courage. Perhaps courage is a basic life quality which God gives us, since it is of spirit. Moments may come when courage alone shall stand between us and disaster. In the long pull across the years, there will be times when we shall need dogged courage to keep going when the going is hard. And what is the source of such rugged courage? Surely that sense of God's presence when we hear Him say, "I am with you always."

Tuesday March 9

Today at the mall, Marg, Bruce, and I got a real kick out of this notice in the window of an appliance store.

Dear Valued Customer:

In an effort to serve you better, we are eliminating our toll-free phone number and relocating our phone support office to the other side of the Arctic Circle. We have also decided to cut our support staff in half and charge you for the privilege of getting help deciphering our manuals. But we will teach you the ins and outs of our very elaborate voice-mail system during your long-distance call.

We will not charge you for the 20-minute interlude of elevator music interspersed again and again with exciting news of our slower-moving products. Since all our service personnel are tied up with other customers, please feel free to leave your name and number. We will not call you back but, after a suitable length of time, you will grow as a human being by solving your own technical problem.

If our voice-mail system breaks down, and you do get through to a real human being, we want you to know that your call will be recorded in order to provide a future comic interlude for our hard-working staff.

Wednesday March 10

MY grandson Marshall, a lawyer, is some-times involved in court cases with victims of car accidents. People can give the strangest excuses for these accidents. Marshall brought me a list of some today.

"The pedestrian had no idea which direction to run, so I ran over him."

"In an attempt to kill a fly, I drove into a telephone pole."

"I had been driving for 40 years when I fell asleep at the wheel and had an accident."

"To avoid hitting the car in front of me, I struck a pedestrian."

"My mother called me on my brand-new car phone. I was so excited to get a call that I drove into the parked car."

Thursday March 11

SOMETIMES we forget that our year requires four seasons to complete the life cycle. In man's life and in nature, the process is orderly and cannot be hurried. He who feels in tune with the verities knows that winter is a part of life.

Friday March 12

I WAS remembering today my dear friend Betty, who passed away several years ago. For the last years of her life, Betty was completely bedridden—something that could have made her bitter. Instead, she accepted her fate with equanimity, and her sunny, cheerful disposition made her a good friend to many and an inspiration to others.

How does someone who has been dealt such a cruel fate remain happy and optimistic? I think Betty said it best.

"You know, Edna, all of us, at some time or another, wonder 'Why am I here?' When I became ill, and then found that I would be bedridden, I asked myself that question very often. I found that my best answer came when I asked myself not 'What can't I do?' but 'What can I do?' When I started searching for those things that I was still able to do, the list was long. Once I made up my mind to enjoy these things, I never really felt that I had lost very much."

I hope that I would have Betty's courage were I ever in the same situation.

Saturday March 13

THE beautiful thing about the relationship between a man and his dog is that each is thinking that he is taking care of the other.

Bern Williams

Sunday March 14

AND now, my friends, think on all that is lovable, amicable, and deserving love; think on the beauty of the earth, for it was created for love and by love, behold the beauty of the soul, the fullest expression of God's love.

God loved the world so much, that he gave his only son so that everyone who has faith in Him may not die but have eternal life.

Monday March 15

ONE of the hardest lessons we have to learn in this life, and one that many persons never learn, is to see the divine, the celestial, the pure in the common—the near at hand. To see that heaven lies about us here in this world.

John Burroughs

Tuesday March 16

I WAS a great admirer of Erma Bombeck, the American humourist, whose wit and wisdom entertained millions.

Erma wrote books that poked fun at family life, completing more than a dozen before her death from kidney disease. When she needed a transplant, she could have used her "star" status to jump to the top of the list, but in her usual humble fashion she chose to wait quietly—almost two years. Sadly, the transplant didn't take properly, and she died of heart failure April 22, 1996.

I believe that her great appeal came from her extraordinary ability to see the humour in ordinary situations. Somehow, that seemed to make her "one of us." I shall miss this very funny lady.

On weight loss: "I have dieted continuously for the last two decades. By all calculations, I should be hanging from a charm bracelet."

On opportunities: "Seize the moment. Remember all those women on the *Titanic* who waved off the dessert cart."

On marriage: "I have just come up with a wonderful solution to end all wars—let men give directions on how to get there."

Wednesday March 17

As spring approaches, many of us feel the need to begin that yearly ritual—"spring cleaning." For many of us seniors, who may be living in smaller quarters, finding storage space can be a challenge. My friend Muriel has some unique suggestions for finding added storage space.

Pack off-season clothing and linens into boxes and slide them under a bed.

Find a hollow ottoman, bench or window seat with a lift-up top that will give space for many items.

Bulky items can be hidden in a corner by an attractive folding screen.

Wall-mounted decorative baskets are a handy place to keep all manner of smaller items that can clutter countertops or desks.

Thursday March 18

MINE honour is my life; both grow in one; Take honour from me, and my life is done.

William Shakespeare

Friday March 19

THE best help is not to bear the troubles of others for them, but to inspire them with courage and energy, to bear their burdens for themselves and meet the difficulties of life bravely.

John Lubbock

Saturday March 20

WHEN I hear music, I fear no danger, I am invulnerable, I see no foe. I am related to the earliest times and to the latest.

Henry David Thoreau

Sunday March 21

I ATTENDED church this morning with my grandson, Marshall, his wife, Jamie, and their two children, Bethany and Michael. By coincidence, one of the hymns for the morning was directed to the children.

When mothers of Salem their children brought
    to Jesus,
The stern disciples drove them back and bade
    them depart.
But Jesus saw them ere they fled, and sweetly
    smiled and kindly said,
Suffer the little children to come unto Me.

Monday March 22

FOR seven years now, our family has had two reasons to celebrate yesterday. As we revelled in the arrival of spring, we also celebrated the birthday of my great-granddaughter Bethany.

How appropriate, that a child who has such a bright and sunny disposition should have been born on the first day of spring.

The years at the spring
And the days at the morn;
Morning's at seven;
The hillside is dew-pearled;
The larks on the wing;
The snails on the thorn;
God's in his heaven—
All's right with the world!

Robert Browning

Tuesday March 23

THIS morning, I felt the need to bring a little spring into someone's life. What better way to do that than with flowers. My favourite spring flowers are tulips and, as luck would have it, our local grocery store had a selection of potted tulips, in many bright colours.

I chose a beautiful pot of scarlet red tulips, sure to bring a touch of spring to even the rainiest day.

I could hardly wait to present them to my beloved friend and neighbour, Lila MacGuiness. There is such joy in giving something that you know will be appreciated so much.

Wednesday March 24

> For, lo, the winter is past,
> The rain is over and gone;
> The flowers appear on the earth;
> The time of the singing of birds is come,
> And the voice of the turtle is heard in our land.

Song of Solomon 2:11–12

Thursday March 25

IT doesn't take monumental feats to make the world a better place. It can be as simple as letting someone go ahead of us in a grocery line.

Friday March 26

LET the dawn of the morning be to you as the beginning of life, and every setting sun be to you as its close; then let every one of these short lives have its record of some kindly thing done for others, some goodly strength or knowledge gained for yourself.

John Ruskin

Saturday March 27

IWAS born and raised on Canada's East Coast. Whenever I am feeling nostalgic, I pull out my recipe-card box and prepare something that is typical "down home" food. Today's recipe fills the bill!

Great Grandpa's Salt Fish Pie

2 lb. salt cod

2 onions (or more to taste), sliced

3 tomatoes, sliced

curry powder

6 potatoes, cooked and mashed

Soak overnight 2 lb. salt cod. Boil the fish until it flakes easily.

In a well-buttered baking dish, place a layer of the flaked fish. Cover with sliced tomatoes and onions and sprinkle with curry powder. Repeat layers and then cover with the mashed potatoes.

Bake uncovered in a 325-degree oven until the potatoes are browned.

Serves 4.

Sunday March 28

Palm Sunday

LET not your heart be troubled; ye believe in God, believe also in me. In my father's house are many mansions: if it were not so, I would have told you. I go to prepare a place for you.

John 14:1–2

Monday March 29

A SURE sign of spring, for me, is the sighting of the first robin. There is a delightful fable that describes how the robin got his red breast.

According to legend, a robin was in the stable when Jesus was born. While the newborn baby was sleeping, warmed by a small fire, the undistinguished brown-feathered bird watched in awe. Suddenly, the bird noticed that the fire was dying out. The baby would get cold! Flying to the coals, the tiny bird hovered over them and began fanning them with his wings. It was tough work, but the flames were revived. All through the night, whenever the fire dimmed, the bird returned; thus the Christ Child stayed warm. When the sun rose, the tired bird flew off to rest, but his friends were amazed. No longer was he plain brown; now he had a blazing red breast. And that, according to legend, is how the robin won its wonderful marking.

Tuesday March 30

Our lives are songs; God writes the words
And we set them to music at pleasure;
And the song grows glad, or sweet or sad,
As we choose to fashion the measure.

Ella Wheeler Wilcox

Wednesday March 31

DURING Holy Week, I try to attend two or three morning services. This morning Marg joined Lila and me, and we sang a hymn that is perhaps one of the most beloved of any in the hymnal.

Abide with me, fast falls the eventide,
The darkness weakens, Lord with me abide!
When other helpers fail, and comforts flee,
Help of the helpless, O abide with me!

Hold Thou Thy cross before my closing eyes
Shine thru the gloom and point me to the skies:
Heaven's morning breaks, and the earth's vain
    shadows flee;
In life and death, O Lord, abide with me.

William H. Monk

April

Thursday April 1

We are the roadside flowers,
Straying from garden grounds;
Lovers of idle hours,
Breakers of ordered grounds.

If only the earth will feed us,
If only the wind be kind,
We blossom for those who need us,
The stragglers left behind.

And lo, the Lord of the garden,
He makes His sun to rise
And His rain to fall like pardon
On our dusty paradise.

On us He has laid the duty—
The task of the wandering breed—
To better the world with beauty,
Wherever the way may lead.

Who shall inquire of the season,
Or question the wind where it blows?
We blossom and ask no reason,
The Lord of the Garden knows.

Bliss Carman

Friday April 2

Good Friday

AND it was now about the sixth hour, and darkness fell over the whole land until the ninth hour, the sun being obscured; and the veil of the temple was torn in two. And Jesus, crying out with a loud voice, said, "Father, into Thy hands I commit my spirit." And having said this, He breathed his last.

Luke 23:44–46

Saturday April 3

READING books in one's youth is like looking at the moon through a crevice; reading books in middle age is like looking at the moon in one's courtyard; and reading books in old age is like looking at the moon on an open terrace. This is because the depths of benefits of reading varies in proportion to the depths of one's own experience.

Chang Ch'as

Sunday April 4

Easter Sunday

"JESUS Christ is risen today. Hallelujah. He is risen indeed. Hallelujah."

May the joy of Easter be with you today and always.

Monday April 5

DR. Abraham Gesner was a Canadian genius who worked for his lifetime to give the world "a light for the night."

Born in Cornwallis, Nova Scotia, Abraham had a fascination for rocks, minerals, and fossils. His many experiments led him on a quest to produce a light that would be cheap, safe, and bright.

Dr. Gesner unveiled his discovery in 1846, in Charlottetown, P.E.I. He called his product "kerosene," from the Greek words *keros* meaning wax and *elaion* meaning oil. He had developed the process of distillation of kerosene from hydrocarbons and, on that evening, when he lit a match, the flame that the fuel produced was brighter than any other.

Kerosene replaced whale oil as the major domestic lighting fuel, and his distillation process was later used to refine the first barrels of North American crude oil. Although Gesner was the father of the modern petroleum industry, recognition was not forthcoming until some 70 years after his death, when Imperial Oil placed a marble obelisk on his grave in Halifax, "as a token of appreciation.... for his contribution to the oil industry." It is a small, but well-deserved, memorial.

Tuesday April 6

IN the airport at Auckland, New Zealand, there are two quotations written on the walls at either end of the building. I liked them so much that I copied them on a scrap of paper to share with you.

Every flyer who ventured across oceans to distant lands is a potential explorer; in his or her breast burns the same fire that urged adventurers of old to set forth on their sailing ships for foreign lands.

Jean Batten 1979
"Alone in the Sky"

For I dipt into the future,
Far as human eyes could see,
Saw the vision of the world,
And all the wonder that would be;
Saw the heavens fill with commerce,
Argosies of magic sails,
Pilots of the purple twilight,
Dropping down the costly bales.

Lord Alfred Tennyson
"Locksley Hall"

Wednesday April 7

THE light of friendship is like the light of phosphorus, seen when all around is dark.

Thursday April 8

SOME friends and I were discussing a problem that seems to be quite common. A large percentage of our population suffers from some form of sleeping difficulty.

In the younger set, insomnia, and the problems it can cause on the job, costs millions of dollars annually. For those of us who are seniors, lack of sleep can cause dizziness and potential injuries from falls.

My friend Mildred read an article recently that suggests that certain foods can be a wonderful sleep aid. Foods that contain the amino acid tryptophan help induce sleep, and the trick is to find the foods that work best for you.

Some of the foods that may help you get a good night's sleep are tuna fish, cottage cheese, peanut butter, bananas, warm milk, white rice, turkey, and yogurt.

Not everything will work for everyone, but a little experimentation should help you to find your best combination.

Friday April 9

FLATTER me and I may not believe you. Criticize me, and I may not forgive you. Encourage me, and I will not forget you.

W. A. Ward

Saturday April 10

MY daughter Julia answered the telephone in her husband's office with, "I'm sorry, but the doctor is out right now. Would you like to leave a message?"

The voice on the other end replied, "Yes."

Julia waited patiently, and then repeated, "Do you want to leave a message?"

There was a pause on the other end before a voice asked "Aren't you a recording?"

"No, I'm afraid I'm a real person," replied Julia.

"For heaven's sake. I was waiting for you to beep," said the caller with a laugh.

Sunday April 11

ALMIGHTY Father, who hast given thine only Son to die for our sins, and to rise again for our justification: Grant us so to put away the leaven of malice and wickedness, that we may always serve thee in pureness of living and truth; through the merits of the same thy Son Jesus Christ our Lord. Amen.

The Book of Common Prayer

Monday April 12

ISN'T it strange how some small thing will trigger a memory that seemed long forgotten?

A snatch of music, heard on the radio this morning, reminded me of the travelling organ grinder and his little monkey that, as children, Sarah, Ben, and I adored.

We could hear the music from blocks away, but mother insisted that we wait until they arrived on our street before we tried to get close. We would sit on the steps of the porch, watching anxiously, until they came into view.

Mr. Tony carried his music box on a leather strap that hung over his shoulder and around his neck. Pepi, his monkey, was dressed in a bright red jacket with gold trim and shiny brass buttons. His red pillbox hat, and his black harness and leash completed his ensemble.

When Tony stopped to crank the music, Pepi would stand on the sidewalk and dance from child to child. Children who had coins for the monkey were rewarded with a handshake and a doffed cap before the coins were squirrelled away in his tiny pockets.

Their visits brought something special to our lives, and gave me this happy memory many years later.

Tuesday April 13

YOUNG people searching for their "real self" must learn that the real self is not something one finds as much as it is something one makes; and it is one's daily actions that shape the inner personality far more permanently than any amount of introspection or intellection.

Sydney J. Harris

Wednesday April 14

MY son-in-law, Bruce, wages an ongoing "battle of the bulge." Each year, about this time, he pulls out his spring and summer wardrobe and complains that his clothing must have shrunk over the winter. Then he concedes that it is possible that he may have put on just a "tiny bit of weight" over the winter, and perhaps we should cut back on desserts. This cutback lasts about a week (a week filled with much whining), before Bruce buys several new pairs of pants to wear "just until I am my svelte self again."

This spring, Bruce has changed his strategy. He came home this afternoon and announced that he had solved his weight problem.

"I purchased a metric scale, and now I have absolutely no idea what I weigh!"

Thursday April 15

ONE of the biggest thrills in life comes from doing a job well.

Friday April 16

MY friend Jake told me this story of Mark Twain, one of my favourite authors.

Once, when Mark Twain was lecturing in Utah, a Mormon acquaintance argued with him on the subject of polygamy. The two debated at length until finally the Mormon said, "Can you find any place in the scriptures that forbids polygamy?"

Twain thought for a moment and then answered, "Certainly sir—no man can serve two masters."

Saturday April 17

THE proliferation of garage sales leads us to suspect that the whole economy is sustained by everybody buying everybody else's junk.

Bill Vaughan

Sunday April 18

WHAT doth the Lord thy God require of thee, but to fear the Lord thy God, to walk in all His ways, and to love Him, and to serve the Lord thy God with all thy heart and with all thy soul?

Deuteronomy 10:12

Monday April 19

IS there anything more lovely than a long walk on a warm spring day? My friend Lila and I took advantage of the change in temperature to look for signs that spring has indeed arrived.

Come, fill the Cup, and in the fire of Spring,
The Winter garment of Repentance fling:
The bird of Time has but a little way
To fly—and Lo! the Bird is on the wing.

Edward Fitzgerald

Tuesday April 20

IN keeping with Bruce's efforts at weight loss, Marg has come up with a delicious recipe for spinach-cheese pasta. When prepared with yolk-free noodles, this pasta is completely fat free. It makes a delicious side dish to serve with grilled fish or chicken.

Spinach-Cheese Pasta

16 oz. yolk-free noodles

2 tsp. minced garlic

2 (10 oz.) packages frozen chopped spinach,
thawed and drained

1/2 tsp. onion powder

1/2 tsp. dried basil

1 cup fat-free ricotta cheese

salt and pepper to taste

1/4 cup fat-free Parmesan cheese

Cook noodles according to the package directions. Drain well; keep warm.

Lightly spray a large skillet with non-fat cooking spray and heat over medium-high heat. Add the garlic and spinach. Cook about 5 minutes, until softened.

Add onion powder, basil, ricotta cheese, salt and pepper. Cook over low heat, stirring frequently until mixture is blended and heated through.

In a large serving bowl, toss spinach mixture with cooked noodles. Sprinkle with Parmesan cheese. Serves 8. 253 calories per serving.

Wednesday April 21

THE books which help you most are those which make you think the most. The hardest way of learning is by easy reading; but a great book which comes from a great thinker—it is a ship of thought, deep freighted with truth and with beauty.

Theodore Parker

Thursday April 22

CHRISTIAN faith is a grand cathedral, with divinely pictured windows. Standing without, you can see no glory, nor can imagine any, but standing within, every ray of light reveals a harmony of unspeakable splendours.

Nathaniel Hawthorne

Friday April 23

IF envy were not such a tearing thing to feel, it would be the most comic of sins. It is usually, if not always, based on a complete misunderstanding of another person's situation.

Monica Furlong

Saturday April 24

MY friend Marcia, who lives in Boston, wrote to me: "There is a group of volunteers at the Beth Abraham Health Services in New York City that are known as the Golden Gals. They are simply wonderful, Edna. Most are well into their 80s, but, as one volunteer said, 'I just can't see myself sitting at home in a rocking chair, watching television.' These ladies spend hundreds of hours each year performing such tasks as reading aloud, letter writing, watering plants or pushing wheelchairs.

"The Golden Gals are well able to relate to the residents. They know what it is like to age—many have lost husbands and dear friends, and some of the Golden Gals have health problems of their own.

"I think that this would be a wonderful program to start in many places, don't you? I'll bet we both know many women and men who would like to contribute in this way."

Sometimes, we seniors seem to forget what a valuable commodity we really are. We have free time that we didn't have when we were younger. We also have the empathy to relate to seniors who are less able than we are to perform these much-needed tasks. Then too, there is something wonderful about being needed.

Tuesday May 4

There's one sad truth in life I found
While journeying east to west,
The only folks we really wound
Are those we love the best.
We flatter those we scarcely know,
We please the fleeting guest,
And deal full many a thoughtless blow
To those who love us best.

Wednesday May 5

IF we work on marble, it will perish; if we work upon brass, time will efface it; if we rear temples, they will crumble into dust; but if we work upon immortal souls, if we imbue them with principles, with the just fear of the Creator and love of fellow men, we will engrave on those tablets something which will brighten all eternity.

Daniel Webster

Thursday May 6

WHEN I go to the grave I can say as others have said, "My day's work is done." But I cannot say, "My life is done." My day's work will recommence the next morning. The tomb is not a blind alley; it is a thoroughfare. It closes upon the twilight, but opens upon the dawn.

Victor Hugo

Friday May 7

THOSE who know the path to God can find it in the dark.

Ian MacLaren

Saturday May 8

TO keep the heart unwrinkled, to be hopeful, kindly, cheerful, reverent; that is to triumph over old age.

Thomas Bailey Aldrich

Sunday May 9

Mother's Day

She always leaned to watch for us,
Anxious if we were late,
In winter by the window,
In summer by the gate;

And though we mocked her tenderly,
Who had such foolish care,
The long way home would seem more safe
Because she waited there.

Her thoughts were all so full of us,
She never could forget!
And so I think that where she is
She must be watching,

Waiting till we come home to her,
Anxious if we are late—
Watching from Heaven's window,
Leaning from Heaven's gate.

Margaret Widdemer

Monday May 10

FORTUNATE is the person who shares a happy family and home life. I am one of those lucky people, and I give thanks each day for my wonderful relations and the love and laughter that has always been a part of my life.

Where we love is home. Home is where our feet may leave but not our hearts.

Oliver Wendell Holmes

But every house where Love abides
And Friendship is a guest,
Is surely home, and home, sweet home;
For there the heart can rest.

Henry van Dyke

The home is the centre and circumference, the start and the finish, of most of our lives.

Charlotte Perkins Gilman

But what on earth is half so dear—so longed for as the hearth of home?

Emily Brontë

Home is the one place in all this world where hearts are sure of each other.

Frederick Robertson

Tuesday May 11

WHO can bear to throw out an old teapot? My teapots have so many memories that I can never be persuaded to get rid of them.

My sister Sarah sent along these suggestions in her letter today and I can hardly wait to try them.

"I found a number of old teapots in the cupboard that had chipped spouts or a cracked base. They were still quite lovely so I really didn't want to throw them away.

"I filled one of them with water and put in some ivy. In no time the ivy had grown roots and was trailing very prettily across the table.

"In another I am growing watercress which I hope to use in watercress sandwiches for afternoon tea.

"In a plain white china teapot I put a layer of charcoal and then I filled it with good potting soil and planted a beautiful purple African violet.

"These teapots really felt like old friends, so I was happy to find a new use for them."

Wednesday May 12

TREAT your friends like family and your family like friends.

Thursday May 13

Ascension Day

GRANT, we beseech thee, Almighty God, that like as we do believe Thy only begotten Son our Lord Jesus Christ to have ascended into the heavens; so we may also in heart and mind thither ascend, and with him continually dwell; who liveth and reigneth with thee and the Holy Spirit, one God, world without end. Amen.

The Book of Common Prayer

Friday May 14

HOW important is a spirit of cooperation?

On a street in China there were two houses in which people had to eat with chopsticks five feet long. In both houses the tables were loaded with fine foods. In one house the people argued, pushed, and shoved as they tried to eat with the gigantic chopsticks.

In the other house everything was peaceful. Everyone was happy and well fed. What was the secret? They used the long chopsticks to feed each other.

Saturday May 15

ONE of the things that I enjoy most when the warm weather arrives is a barbecued dinner.

Grilled Sirloin Steaks with Blue Cheese Walnut Butter

6 oz. blue cheese, crumbled (about 1 1/3 cups)

4 tbsp. butter, room temperature

2 tbsp. chopped fresh parsley

3/4 tsp. + 1 tbsp. dried rosemary, finely crumbled

1/4 cup chopped toasted walnuts (about 1 oz.)

6 large cloves of garlic, peeled

1 1/2 tsp. each ground black pepper and salt

2 lb. top sirloin steaks (about 1 inch thick)

In a medium bowl, combine cheese, butter, parsley, and 3/4 tsp. rosemary. Stir to blend well. Mix in walnuts. Season to taste with salt and pepper. Transfer mixture to a small bowl. Cover and refrigerate. Bring to room temperature before serving. Combine 1 tbsp. rosemary, garlic, pepper (and salt if you wish) in a processor. Blend until mixture resembles coarse paste. Pat steaks dry. Place in large baking dish. Rub 2 tsp. of garlic paste on each side of each steak. Cover and let stand 1 hour at room temperature. Place on barbecue (medium-high heat). Grill steaks to desired doneness. Transfer steaks to a platter; let stand 5 min. Cut each steak into 3 equal portions. Top each portion with a spoonful of the blue cheese butter and serve. Leftover butter is delicious on baked potatoes or French bread.

Serves 6.

Sunday May 16

O GOD the King of glory, who hast exalted thine only Son Jesus Christ with great triumph into thy kingdom of heaven: We beseech thee, leave us not comfortless; but send to us thine Holy Ghost to comfort us, and exalt us unto the same place whither our Saviour Christ is gone before; who liveth and reigneth with thee and the Holy Ghost, one God, world without end. Amen.

Monday May 17

N ATURE is man's teacher. She unfolds her treasures to his search, unseals his eye, illumes his mind, and purifies his heart; and influence breathes from all the sights and sounds of her existence.

Tuesday May 18

IN three words I can sum up everything I've learned about life. It goes on.

Wednesday May 19

THIS is the time of year when young people are hunting for summer employment. My grandson Fred found these words of wisdom to offer to his sons.

Do your best, not because your work is worth it, but because you are. Whatever you are doing, you are making manhood. Half-hearted work makes only half a man. Slipshod methods mean loose principles. The only way to keep character up to the standard is by continually living up to the highest standard in all that you do.

Thursday May 20

SOMETIMES we look on famous men and women as persons born with special talents, unique skills or unusual intellect. In fact, however, many were not particularly outstanding among their peers until they found their place, their calling.

Thomas Edison was once at the bottom of his class, and yet his inventions are considered to be some of the most brilliant of his time.

Albert Einstein flunked math and was called "mentally slow," and Henry Ford was written off by one of his teachers as "a student who shows no promise."

Each of us has special God-given gifts, but not all are equally successful at discovering or using them.

Friday May 21

THE trouble with giving advice is that others want to return the favour.

Saturday May 22

THIS is the first long weekend of the cottage season, and, as we have done for many years, we are assisting my dear friend Eleanor with the chore of opening up her summer home.

When Eleanor's husband Bob passed away many years ago, the task of opening up the cottage seemed overwhelming to her. My son-in-law Bruce offered to help Eleanor that first year, and it has become an annual event.

When I think back to the "good old days," when George and I used to rent a cottage, I have to laugh. When we were young, such peccadilloes as outdoor plumbing, a leaky roof, or cold-water washing seemed only to add to the charm. Now, as a senior, I confess that I am happy to enjoy all of the comforts that Eleanor's cottage has to offer.

This weekend, Marg, Bruce, Eleanor, and I will delight in a lovely place to stay, good company, and the sights and sounds that make Muskoka so special.

Sunday May 23

All things bright and beautiful,
All creatures great and small,
All things wise and wonderful,
The Lord God made them all.

Monday May 24

ON this day in 1819, Princess Alexandria Victoria was born in London, England. Daughter of Prince Edward, Duke of Kent, and princess Victoria, she was destined to become Britain's longest-reigning monarch.

On June 28, 1837, just one month after her 18th birthday, Victoria was crowned Queen of England. Her poise, modesty, and common sense made a favourable impression on the nation. She increased her popularity even more by promptly paying her father's debts, which were considerable.

In 1840, Victoria married her 20-year-old cousin, Prince Albert, who was largely responsible for setting the tone of moral earnestness and straight-laced propriety of what would become known as the "Victorian Era."

Queen Victoria's strength lay in her moral fibre and directness of character.

I believe we could use a little more of the Victorian Era's principles in today's world.

Tuesday May 25

YESTERDAY was a holiday for our American neighbours as well. For them it was Memorial Day, the day traditionally set aside to honour those who died in the service of their country.

This excerpt from James Whitcomb Riley's poem "Away" seems an appropriate offering for our friends who live south of the border.

I cannot say, and I will not say
That he is dead. He is just away!
With a cheery smile and a wave of the hand,
He has wandered into an unknown land.
And left us dreaming how very fair
It needs must be, since he lingers there.
Think of him faring on, as dear
In the love of There as the love of Here:
Think of him still the same, I say:
He is not dead—he is just—away!

Wednesday May 26

REJOICE in all the honours which came to those you know. That you know them makes you, in a sense, a partner in their fame; that you rejoice with them brings you their friendship.

Henry Worthington

Thursday May 27

GOOD kids are like sunsets. We take them for granted. Every evening, they disappear. Most parents never imagine how hard they try to please us, and how miserable they feel when they think they have failed.

Erma Bombeck

Friday May 28

WHAT will your children remember? Moments spent listening, talking, playing and sharing together may be the most important times of all.

Gloria Gaither

June

Tuesday June 1

MY husband George and I were married on this day, many years ago. I offer this poem, by Eldredge Denison, today as a tribute to the wonderful man who was my husband.

How far together? Till the road
    Ends at some churchyard wall; until the bell
Tolls for the entrance to the lone abode;
    Until the only whisper is "Farewell"?

How far together? Till the light
    No longer wakens in the loving eyes;
Until the shadow of the final night
    Has swept the last star-glimmer from the
    skies?

How far together? Past the end
    Of this short road, beyond the starry gleam;
Till day and night and time and space shall
    blend
    Into the vast Forever of our Dream.

Wednesday June 2

MY friend Lila made me laugh today. Her minister, in a recent visit, said that at her age she should be thinking about the "hereafter."

"I told him, Edna, that I do, all the time. No matter where I am—in the living room, my bedroom, the kitchen—I say to myself, 'What am I here after?'"

Thursday June 3

BRUCE continues to work hard to lose some unwanted pounds. Marg and I are very proud of his efforts. It's not easy to be committed to his low-fat regimen, particularly when he loves food as much as he does. Even when he barbecues for the family, or some "forbidden" food appears on the dinner table, Bruce chooses to eat only the foods that he knows are low in fat.

Bruce has also added an exercise component to his day, and this, along with his diet, is allowing him to lose weight safely. A healthy diet, plenty of exercise…I guess this is what we all need!

Friday June 4

IN Portland, Oregon, there is a unique "re-cycling" program.

More than 300 bicycles are parked all across the city for anyone to enjoy, and each one bears the message: "Free community bike. Please return to a major street for others to reuse. Use at your own risk."

The free ride program was the brainchild of resident Tom O'Keefe. He collected bicycles that were donated by area residents, the Salvation Army and the Portland Police Department.

A group of helpful citizens keep the bicycles in good repair. The project has been so successful that other cities are starting their own bike-sharing programs.

Saturday June 5

Our deeds will travel
With us from afar,
And what we have been
Makes us what we are.

Sunday June 6

ONE generation passeth away, and another generation cometh; but the earth abideth forever.

Ecclesiastes 1:4

Monday June 7

What is a failure? It's only a spur
To a man who receives it right.
And makes the spirit within him stir
To go in once more and fight.
If you never have failed, it's an even guess,
You never have won a high success.

Edmund Vance Cook

Tuesday June 8

MY grandson Fred and his wife June passed along this story for today.

During the Depression, Nora Sullivan allowed hungry customers to charge their groceries at her store, even though she knew that few would be able to pay her back. When Nora retired, most of the Depression-era charges remained on her books, unpaid.

Some 50 years after her kindness, however, she received a cheque for $100 from the estate of a man who had directed his heirs to repay his debt. When a local newspaper reported the payment, cheques began to pour in from the other grateful customers who wanted to make good on a debt owed to a kind and generous lady.

Wednesday June 9

TODAY I was overwhelmed by an act of kindness that makes this birthday one of the most special in my life.

I have a number of close friends living in our local nursing home. At about 11 o'clock this morning, three limousines arrived at the home to pick up 11 of them. At the same time, a limousine arrived at our home to pick up Marg, Mary, Julia, and me. I can't tell you how surprised I was when I learned that my daughters, my friends, and I were being treated to a wonderful drive, in magnificent cars, to the Millcroft Inn, in Alton.

There, we were seated in the beautiful dining room overlooking the falls, where we enjoyed an exquisite lunch.

A birthday card signed by many of my friends and relatives explained:

"This year, Edna, we decided that we wanted to give you something different that we knew you would enjoy. Time spent with family and friends is so important to you, so what better way to celebrate a birthday than with a few of both.

"Happy Birthday, with love from all of us!"

Thursday June 10

M ANY times a day, I realize how much my own outer and inner life is built upon the labours of my fellow men, both living and dead, and how earnestly I must exert myself in order to give in return as much as I have received.

Albert Einstein

Friday June 11

M Y granddaughter Phyllis, her daughter Jenny, and I were shopping a short while ago when a severe thunderstorm caused a power outage. We happened to be in a large mall at the time, and, although the power was only off for a few hours, it caused chaos.

Emergency generators kept some lights on in the core of the mall, but for the most part, it was extremely dark. Banks were forced to shut down because the computers were not functional. Stores could not sell their goods because the tills would not open without power.

Many years ago, this would not have been a problem. Many shopkeepers considered electricity to be unreliable, and their stores had their own oil lamps or candles in case the power should go off unexpectedly. Bank tellers all had their own cash drawers, and all transactions were hand written. No power? No problem.

Saturday June 12

THERE is probably nothing more shattering than the loss of a child.

Reg and Maggie Green, of Bodega Bay, a small fishing village north of San Francisco, loved to travel with their children, Nicholas and Eleanor. On the night of September 29, 1994, the family was driving in Italy when a car pulled alongside them on a deserted stretch of highway. There was a loud bang, and the back-seat window shattered. A second shot splintered the driver's side window. Reg accelerated and drove like a demon to outrun the assailants. Maggie checked the back seat and was relieved to see the children still sleeping. Only minutes later did they realize that Nicholas had been shot in the head. Two endless days later, doctors gave them the devastating news that Nicholas was brain dead.

The shooting was a page-one newspaper story, as was the family's decision to donate Nicholas' organs. The end of this little boy's life marked an international surge in organ donations—the number in Italy alone increased by 400% in the month after his death.

Because of this family's courage, many others will be considering lifesaving donations.

Sunday June 13

I LOVE the Lord, because he hath heard my voice and my supplications. Because He hath inclined his ear unto me, therefore will I call upon Him as long as I live.

Psalms 116:1–2

Monday June 14

A S we come to the end of another school year, I know that I shall miss my "reading buddies." Both Marg and I have been involved in the "Grandtimers" program in our local school, and have enjoyed it immensely.

Senior citizens are asked to come to the school to read to children of all grade levels. Volunteers work with the same children each week. A wonderful bond forms, and the children not only enjoy their time of reading, they often look upon their partner as a friend and confidante.

Most gratifying to me have been the strides made by Matt, who was a very difficult child at the year's beginning. His face, once a sullen mask, now radiates happiness and confidence, and his cheerful, "Thanks a lot, Mrs. McCann!" makes the effort all the more worthwhile.

Tuesday June 15

CHAMPIONS aren't made in gyms. Champions are made from something they have deep inside them—a desire, a dream, a vision. They have to have last-minute stamina, they have to be a little faster, they have to have the skill and the will. But the will must be stronger than the skill.

Muhammad Ali

Wednesday June 16

IT is curious that physical courage should be so common in the world and moral courage so rare.

Mark Twain

Thursday June 17

THE greatest gift that has come to me is the affection of so many—far more important than people feeling sorry for me. In fact, feeling sorry for someone is simply to give him a pain reliever. Love is a healing force.

Hubert H. Humphrey
(shortly before he died from cancer)

Friday June 18

MY good friend Ethel is one of those people who seems to have the happy knack of always finding a bargain. I asked her to tell me the secret of her success and was surprised that her suggestions seemed so simple.

"These days, it's pretty easy to get a bargain. Because of the competition, even the most exclusive stores are willing to haggle over the price of everything from appliances to jewellery to clothing—even vacations. I regularly ask, 'Can you do any better?' and this simple question often results in a reduction of 10 or even 20% off the price shown on the ticket.

"You may also offer to buy a floor model or a style that is discontinued. The shop owners are often very happy to give a particularly good price on such items.

"Another way to do well is to ask the merchant to add in some accessories. I bought a new vacuum cleaner for a price that was a little more than I wanted to spend, but when I said, 'would you include the extra-long hose, some filter bags, and the attachments?' the salesman was quick to oblige.

I believe I will have to try her suggestions (and hope for her success).

one; for nature and grace are one—grace the heart of the flower, and nature its surrounding petals.

Henry Ward Beecher

Wednesday June 30

Because Marg and I have spent some time at our local school, a number of the youngsters feel comfortable stopping in for a glass of lemonade and cookies. I look forward to their visits with unbridled enthusiasm. Hearing their stories and watching their never-ending energy gives me a real lift on a warm summer's day.

If you feel the need of a "pick-me-up," invite some of your young neighbours over for a visit. I guarantee you won't be disappointed.

July

Thursday July 1

Canada Day

O NE hundred and thirty-two years ago, with the signing of the Articles of Confederation, this majestic country of Canada that we call home came into being.

Someone once said, "A nation is a body of people who have done great things together in the past and hope to do great things together in the future."

Canada is such a nation. Treasure it forever.

Friday July 2

T HERE is a feeling among sailors that borders on fatalism. It is born of the belief that a ship can never get lost. When you run out of water, you always run into land. It may not be the right land; but then if it were, America would still be undiscovered.

Robert F. Mirvish in
"There You Are, But Where Are You"

It was because of Guy Weadick's dream that the Calgary Stampede was born, and now, 87 years later, the world's professional cowboys gather this week in Calgary, Alberta, to compete for hundreds of thousands of dollars during the ten-day event.

The friendly people of Calgary will make you welcome, and I know that you will enjoy a look at the skills needed by our country's early settlers.

Saturday July 17

A MEMORY without blot or contamination must be an exquisite treasure, an inexhaustible source of pure refreshment.

Charlotte Brontë

Sunday July 18

B UT thanks be to God, which giveth us the victory through our Lord, Jesus Christ.

Therefore, my beloved brethren, be ye steadfast, unmovable, always abounding in the work of the Lord, forasmuch as ye know that your labour is not in vain in the Lord.

I Corinthians 15:57–58

Monday July 19

BILL Cosby, the legendary American comic, has a new career—as an author. Cosby has written a series of "Little Bill" children's books that he hopes will help young children enjoy learning to read.

Cosby's son Ennis had a learning disability which made reading very difficult for him. He overcame his disability and graduated from college, but tragically, he was murdered in Los Angeles several years ago.

It is to his son that Bill Cosby dedicates these books with the poignant words, "To Ennis, Hello friend."

Tuesday July 20

WHEN my husband George passed away, we received literally hundreds of tributes that came from his many friends and parishioners. Some of these were brilliantly articulated, while others were from "just plain folk" who hoped to lessen our grief.

The tribute that I remember best, however, came from a very old gentleman, who gripped my hands firmly in his and said, "Mrs. McCann, your husband was a kind man."

While Spock was in private practice and teaching pediatrics at Cornell University, he was approached by a publisher to write a paperback book that discussed a new, relaxed style of parenting.

The result was the book that sold more than 50 million copies and made the name "Dr. Spock" synonymous with responsible parenting. His death in March of 1998 came just two months before the seventh revised edition of his legendary book was to be released.

Tuesday July 27

THERE is a passion for perfection which you will rarely see fully developed; but you may note this fact, that in successful lives, it is never wholly lacking.

Bliss Carman

Wednesday July 28

MY garden, with its silence and the pulses of fragrance that come and go on the airy undulations, affects me like sweet music. Care stops at the gates, and gazes at me wistfully through the bars. Among my flowers and trees, Nature takes me into her own hands, and I breathe freely as the first man.

Alexander Smith

Thursday July 29

IF a friend is in trouble, don't annoy him by asking if there is anything you can do. Think up something appropriate, and do it.

Edgar Watson Howe

Friday July 30

THE secret of happiness is not in doing what one likes, but in liking what one has to do.

James M. Barrie

Saturday July 31

DURING the last weekend in July, Mennonites in Manitoba celebrate their heritage. Members of an evangelical Protestant sect originating in Europe, the Mennonites began emigrating to North America in the late 17th century.

Because Mennonites were the first to extract oil from sunflower plants, it seems fitting that the city of Altona celebrates its Mennonite heritage with the Sunflower Festival.

My friend, Mavis Tewsbury, has enjoyed many visits to this unique festival, and each year she seems to find something more to learn about this most interesting group of Canadians.

Friday August 6

ENTRENCHED as we are in the heat of the summer, I often like to enjoy a refreshing bath as a "heat beater."

I find that a cup of lemon juice in the water is particularly refreshing in hot weather, and if you have spent too much time in the sun, one cup of apple cider vinegar will soothe a sunburn.

Saturday August 7

I HAVE arrived here in Muskoka for my annual summer visit with my dear friend Eleanor.

Eleanor and I have known great joys—the births of children and grandchildren and great-grandchildren, and great sorrows—the loss of a husband, family members, and friends. In good times and in bad, we have always been there for each other, to share in the happy times and to provide support in times of crisis. There is nothing that I couldn't tell to Eleanor, nor she to me.

Some people will never enjoy such a friendship. I feel truly blessed that I have such a friend, and our time together here in Muskoka will be added to my precious memories.

Sunday August 8

What a friend we have in Jesus,
All our sins and grief to bear!
What a privilege to carry
Everything to God in prayer!
O what peace we often forfeit,
O what needless pain we bear,
All because we do not carry
Everything to God in prayer!

Joseph Scriven

Monday August 9

HERE in Muskoka, good fish is something we enjoy very much. Eleanor was able to find smoked trout at the farmer's market, and her recipe for pasta with smoked trout and chives is simple but delicious.

1 16-oz. pkg. medium shell pasta (or linguini)
salt (as directed on the pasta package)
12 oz. fresh green beans, trimmed
1 whole smoked trout (about 8 oz.)
1/2 cup half and half light cream
1/2 tsp. grated lemon peel
1/4 tsp. coarsely ground black pepper
4 tbsp. chopped fresh chives
fresh chives for garnish

In a large saucepan, prepare pasta in boiling salted water as the label directs. If you like, cut the green beans crosswise in half. After the pasta has cooked 5 minutes, add the green beans to the pasta in the boiling water and continue to cook until the pasta and the beans are done.

Meanwhile, remove head, tail, skin, and bones from the trout and discard. Separate the flesh into one-inch pieces. In a 2-quart saucepan, heat the half and half, lemon peel, pepper, 1 tbsp. chopped chives, and 1/4 tsp. salt (if desired) over low heat to simmering. Remove the saucepan from the heat and cover to keep warm. When the pasta and beans are cooked to desired doneness, remove 1/2 cup of the pasta cooking water and reserve. Drain the pasta and beans and return to the saucepan. Add half and half mixture, trout, reserved pasta water, and remaining 3 tbsp. chopped chives. Garnish with chives. Makes 6 main-dish servings.

Tuesday August 10

THE body is not a permanent dwelling, but a sort of inn (with a brief sojourn at that), which is to be left behind when one perceives that one is a burden to the host.

Seneca

Wednesday August 11

ELEANOR and I sat on the porch this evening and watched as the moon rose over the pine tree on the far side of the lake. I was reminded of the lovely poem "Silver," by Walter de la Mare.

Slowly, silently, now the moon
Walks the night in her silver shoon;
This way, and that, she peers, and sees
Silver fruit upon silver trees;
One by one the casements catch
Her beams beneath the silvery thatch;
Couched in his kennel, like a log,
With paws of silver sleeps the dog;
From their shadowy cote the white breasts peep
Of doves in a silver-feathered sleep;
A harvest mouse goes scampering by,
With silver claws, and silver eye;
And moveless fish in the water gleam;
By silver reeds in a silver stream.

Thursday August 12

ONE evil in old age is that, as your time is come, you think every little illness the beginning of the end. When a man expects to be arrested, every knock at the door is an alarm.

Sydney Smith

Friday August 13

AT the risk of sounding like a cranky old lady, I feel that the time has come for many parents to teach their children better manners.

Today, for example, Eleanor and I ran into a cottage neighbour and her young son in the grocery store. We three adults were having a brief discussion when Kevin interrupted in a loud voice, "Mom, Mom!" When the mother failed to respond, he pulled on her arm and shouted even louder, "MOM!"

At that point his mother could have responded with an appropriate comment such as, "Just a minute please, Kevin, I'm speaking at the moment and I'll talk to you shortly." Instead, she stopped in mid-sentence and attended to Kevin's wishes.

I don't believe that she is doing Kevin (or herself) a favour by allowing this rude behaviour. Perhaps I am showing my age, but I think not.

Saturday August 14

The old believe everything;
The middle-aged suspect everything;
The young know everything.

Oscar Wilde

Sunday August 15

WE attended the service of worship this morning at the lovely old church at Beaumaris. The sun shone through the beautiful stained-glass windows as we sang:

Breathe on me, Breath of God,
Fill me with life anew,
That I might love what Thou dost love,
And do what Thou wouldst do.

Breathe on me, Breath of God,
Till I am wholly Thine,
Until this earthly part of me
Glows with Thy fire divine.

Reverend Edwin Hatch

Monday August 16

SO live—decently, fearlessly, joyously—and don't forget that in the long run, it is not the years in your life but the life in your years that counts.
Adlai E. Stevenson

Tuesday August 17

OVER lunch today, we discussed a wonderful program that we heard about from my friend Emily. "Grandtravel" offers a variety of tours for children 6–14 years of age and their grandparents.

Emily and her great-granddaughter Kelly recently took advantage of a Special Expedition trip to Sweden.

As Emily explained, "This truly was the vacation of a lifetime for me. Although Kelly and I see each other very often, this was the first time we had spent a longer period of time together, just the two of us. We would stay up talking long into the night, and I really got to know Kelly as I had not known her before. I believe that we will forever have a special relationship as a result of this trip."

We all agreed that this sounds like a unique experience.

Wednesday August 18

O^N the wall in Eleanor's cottage is this "Mother's Blessing."

May the sun stream in your windows,
May your door be busy welcoming good friends,
May your rooms resound with laughter,
May your nights hold sweetest dreams,
And may God's love always fill your heart and home.

Thursday August 19

> Man strives for glory, honour, fame,
> That all the world may know his name.
> Amasses wealth by brain and hand;
> Becomes a power in the land.
> But when he nears the end of life,
> And looks back o'er the years of strife,
> He finds that happiness depends
> On none of these, but love of friends.

Friday August 20

FRIDAY is the day that cottage country comes to life. During the week, the lake is relatively quiet. The boats travel at a leisurely pace; the fishermen stand for long hours casting into the quiet waters; the sound of the loons can be heard at night.

All this changes on Friday, as the weekenders arrive, ready to relax, yet seemingly unable to let go of their mid-week pace.

Thankfully, it all changes back on Saturday morning, and cottage country again becomes a haven for the work weary, and a good place to rest.

Saturday August 21

AS I ready myself to leave for home tomorrow, I like to pause and reflect on the memories that I will take with me from cottage country.

The best memory that I take home with me is of the time spent in the company of a dearly beloved friend.

"If you have one true friend you have more than your share."

Thomas Fuller

Sunday August 22

Immortal, invisible,
God only wise,
In light inaccessible
Hid from our eyes,
Most blessed, most glorious,
The Ancient of Days,
Almighty, victorious—
Thy great name we praise.

Walter Chalmers Smith

Monday August 23

THE years between fifty and seventy are the hardest. You are always being asked to do things, and yet you are not decrepit enough to turn them down.

T. S. Eliot

Tuesday August 24

I AM always amazed by the advances being made in the world of technology.

Parents may now see how their children are doing in daycare—even if they are miles away. Thanks to a new online monitoring service that sends video images from day-care centres to a Web site, parents who have a computer with Internet access can see their children whenever they wish.

Apparently the system is being very well received by the day-care operators, their teachers and the parents alike. It's probably the next best thing to being with them.

Wednesday August 25

O NE doesn't discover new lands without consenting to lose sight of the shore for a very long time.

André Gide

Thursday August 26

T HERE are two lasting bequests we can hope to give our children. One of these is roots; the other wings.

Hodding Carter

Friday August 27

JAMIE stopped by today with young Michael. While he slept, she helped me reorganize my kitchen to make it safer and more efficient. Just a few changes can make a big difference, particularly for a senior such as me.

I am so very grateful for all of the help given me by my wonderful family!

Saturday August 28

THE quality of a person's life is in direct proportion to their commitment to excellence, regardless of their chosen field of endeavour.

Vince Lombardi

Sunday August 29

O worship the King, all glorious above,
And gratefully sing His power and love:
Our Shield and Defender, the Ancient of Days,
Pavilioned in splendour, and girded with praise.
Frail children of dust, and feeble as frail,
In Thee do we trust, nor find Thee to fail:
Thy mercies how tender, how firm to the end,
Our Maker, Defender, Redeemer and Friend.

Sir Robert Grant

Monday August 30

MAN'S mind, once stretched by a new idea, never regains its original dimension.

Oliver Wendell Holmes

Tuesday August 31

Make new friends, but keep the old;
Those are silver, these are gold.
New made friendships, like new wine,
Age will mellow and refine.
Friendships that have stood the test—
Time and change—are surely best;
Brow may wrinkle, hair grow gray,
Friendship never knows decay.
For 'mid old friends, tried and true,
Once more we our youth renew.
But old friends, alas, may die,
New friends must their place supply.
Cherish friendship in your breast—
New is good, but old is best;
Make new friends, but keep the old;
Those are silver, these are gold.

J. Parry

September

Wednesday September 1

"Harvest of the Years"

This is the harvest
   that my hands have garnered
Slowly and patiently
   through the years:

A globe of wisdom
   plucked from high branches,
A cluster of courage
   gathered through tears,

Bright berries of laughter
   tangled with brambles
Humility gained
   from the bitterest fruit—

The years have yielded
   a bountiful harvest
And tangy and sweet
   is my hoarded loot.

Grace Noll Crowell

Thursday September 2

HAVE patience with all things, but chiefly have patience with yourself. Do not lose courage in considering your own imperfections, but instantly set about remedying them—every day begin the task anew.

St. Francis De Sales

Friday September 3

AS we head into the last long weekend before the start of school, I offer these wise words of Howard G. Hendricks, on education.

"It takes at least a couple of decades to realize that you were well taught. All true education is a delayed action bomb assembled in the classrooms for explosion at a later date. An educational fuse fifty years long is by no means unusual."

Saturday September 4

FRIENDS are necessary to a happy life. When friendship deserts us we are as lonely and helpless as a ship, left by the high tide upon the shore. When friendship returns to us, it is as though the tide came back, gave us buoyancy and freedom, and opened to us the wide places of the world.

Harry Emerson Fosdick

Sunday September 5

WISDOM exalteth her children, and layeth hold of them that seek her. He that loveth her loveth life.

Ecclesiasticus 4:11–12, The Apocrypha

Monday September 6

Labour Day

THIS holiday, which falls on the first Monday in September, was first celebrated as a national holiday in 1894.

More than 100 years ago, many workers in Canada worked in dreadful conditions for ridiculously low wages. Particularly affected by this situation were the new immigrants who, wanting to make a new life for themselves, were forced to take any job that was available. Unions were desperately needed to protect the rights of the workers, but at that time unions were illegal.

In 1872, as a result of a city-wide printer's strike in Toronto, the federal government passed legislation that gave official recognition to the trade-union movement. It was a tremendous break-through for the workers and their union leaders.

As a tribute to their political strength and solidarity, the unions organized annual parades and, in 1888, petitioned the federal government for a national day to be known as Labour Day. It wasn't until 1894, however, that it was declared by an act of parliament that the first Monday in September would be Labour Day, and that it would be celebrated as a national holiday.

Tuesday September 7

FOR many students, this is the first day of school. Marg and I enjoyed a cup of tea on the front porch so that we could watch our young neighbours as they headed off to "the halls of learning."

I always find it so interesting to watch the varied reactions of the children as they leave the carefree life of summer vacation.

The very little girls seem to be the most excited and the happiest. They fairly dance down the sidewalk chattering cheerfully with each other, showing off new shoes or hair that is curled in just the latest fashion.

The little boys, for the most part, seem much less anxious to be giving up their time to play. They bounce their tennis balls and catch them in their baseball mitts, all the while hanging back as if hoping the bell will never ring.

The older girls walk together in groups of five or six, and every few minutes they look around to see if any of the young lads are looking in their direction.

The older boys are very busy ignoring the girls, while doing their best to look "cool." Their walk has a bit of a swagger, but occasionally they will forget to be nonchalant and will run off together, pushing and grabbing each other's hats.

I wish the best for all of the students and their teachers.

Wednesday September 8

MY friend Lila and I enjoyed a lovely walk today. Lila uses a wheelchair now, particularly when outdoors. So now, when we visit the neighbourhood, Lila rides and I push. It is an arrangement that is working well for both of us; she gets some fresh air, I get a bit of exercise, and we both enjoy the company and the conversation.

Today, as we passed the high school, we saw that the fall athletic program was in full swing. A tremendous number of young men and women were stretching, in preparation for a cross-country running practice. The football field was littered with young men, running, tackling, kicking or throwing a football. If numbers of players mean anything, it should be an outstanding season!

Thursday September 9

It was in the old frame school house
Our copy books we scanned....
We wrote on smooth, clean pages
In blotless, careful hand.
Those gems of thought we treasured
From childhood's carefree way....
Somehow we can't help feeling
They're just as true today.

Friday September 10

IT'S paradoxical that the idea of living a long life appeals to everyone, but the idea of getting old doesn't appeal to anyone.

Andy Rooney

Saturday September 11

IN a busy world where our work ethic says we must be dedicated, hard workers, it's difficult to imagine that taking breaks would make us more productive—but it is true. A five-minute break, doing something that you enjoy, can have a wonderful rejuvenating effect. The key is to make the break relaxing.

Recall a happy event in your life and replay it in your mind. Look through travel brochures and imagine that you are visiting an exotic location. Look at family albums from a happy occasion.

I am sure that you will come up with your own ideas that will be especially helpful to you.

Sunday September 12

GOD shall wipe away all tears from their eyes; and there shall be no more death, neither sorrow, nor crying, neither shall there be any more pain: for the former things are passed away.

Revelation 21:4

Monday September 13

IF it is not right, do not do it, if it is not true, do not say it.

Marcus Aurelius

Tuesday September 14

MY strong faith gives me hope, at even the darkest hours. No matter what life brings my way, it is my hope for better times that is my guiding light. Many wise people have written of hope and I offer some of their thoughts today.

Hope awakens courage. He who can implant courage in the human soul is the best physician.

Von Knebel

"Hope" is the thing with feathers
That perches in the soul—
And sings the tune without words
And never stops—at all.

Emily Dickinson

Everything that is done in this world is done by
hope.

Martin Luther

Hope ever urges us on, and tells us tomorrow
will be better.

Albius Tibullus

The word that God has written on the brow of
every man is 'hope.'

Victor Hugo

Hope is the dream of a waking man.

Diogenes

Wednesday September 15

IT is a little more than two years now since the
world bade farewell to Diana, the Princess of
Wales, but time does not dim our memory of this
beautiful young woman.

I was a "Diana watcher." I thought that the
Princess was a strikingly beautiful young woman,

and I enjoyed seeing her in her role as a mother. She desperately sought to give her sons a life that was somewhat normal in a world that really never could be so for them, given the circumstances of their birth into royalty.

Diana's death in a car accident, believed by many to have been caused by the paparazzi, sparked an outpouring of grief worldwide, the like of which had never been seen before.

I watched the funeral on television and the sight of her young sons, following the casket, moved me to tears.

Now, two years later, people around the world keep Diana's memory alive by supporting the many charities that were so important to her.

Thursday, September 16

"Age cannot wither her..."

William Shakespeare

Friday September 17

WINNING isn't everything, but wanting to win is.

Vince Lombardi

Saturday September 18

W E are coming to the end of the season for fresh corn. Always one of my favourites, I am forever looking for new recipes that use this delicious vegetable. This recipe for Sunny Corn Muffins gives us a food as attractive as it is tasty.

2 ears fresh corn, with husks
2 tbsp. butter
1/4 cup finely chopped onion
1 cup flour
1 cup yellow cornmeal
2 tsp. baking powder
1 tsp. salt
1/2 tsp. baking soda
1 cup buttermilk
1 large egg
1/4 cup melted butter (or margarine)
1 cup shredded cheddar cheese
1 (4.5-oz.) can chopped green chilies, drained
1/4 cup sunflower kernels

Remove husks from corn; tear the husks into 1/2-inch strips and soak in water 15 minutes. Drain. Cut corn kernels from the cobs. Melt 2 tbsp. butter in a large skillet over medium-high heat; add corn kernels and onion and sauté until tender. Set aside. Combine flour and the next four ingredients in a large bowl. Make a well in the centre of the mixture. Combine buttermilk, egg, and 1/4 cup melted butter; add to dry ingredients, stirring just until moistened. Stir in corn mixture, cheese, and chilies. Arrange four husk strips across each lightly greased muffin cup to resemble spokes; spoon batter into cups, filling each three-quarters full. Sprinkle with sunflower kernels. Bake at 375 degrees for 18–20 minutes or until the muffins are golden brown (corn husks will brown deeply). Remove from pans; cool on a wire rack. To serve, use bamboo skewers as "stems" and serve as a "bouquet" in a decorative vase.

Makes 1 dozen muffins.

Sunday September 19

WHAT doth the Lord require of thee, but to do justly, and to love mercy, and to walk humbly with thy God?

Micah 6:8

Monday September 20

IF a child lives with approval, he learns to live with himself.

Dorothy Law Nolte

Tuesday September 21

Ah, autumn in her passing, leaves
The memory of a lovely song,
And for the heart a legacy
That will last all the winter long.

Wednesday September 22

SO long as we love to serve; so long as we are
loved by others, I would almost say that we
are indispensable; and no man is useless while
he has a friend.

Robert Louis Stevenson

Thursday September 23

WITH these lines from A. Laighton, I welcome
this, the most beautiful season of our year.

"The Richness of Autumn"

The world puts on its robe of glory now—
The very flowers are tinged with deeper dyes;
The waves are bluer and the angels pitch
Their shining tents along the sunset skies.

The distant hills are crowned with purple mist;
The days are mellow, and the long, calm nights,
To wondering eyes, like weird magicians show
The shifting splendours of the northern lights.
The generous earth spreads out her fruitful stores,
And all leaves are thick with ripened sheaves;

While in the woods, at autumn's rustling step,
The birches blush through all their trembling leaves.

Friday September 24

THE autumn brings an abundance of fresh fruits and vegetables. My daughter Mary has a rather different idea for some of the apples.

With her help, we are going to make apple garlands. We pre-heat the oven to 200 degrees, then cut 8 apples into 1/4-inch-thick slices (per garland). We dip the apples into lemon juice and then pat them dry with paper towel. We bake the apple slices on a rack until they are dry and leathery, then we remove them and let them cool.

For each garland we need fine wire, 48 dried apple slices, 16 small (1/2-inch) wooden beads, 9 cinnamon sticks, a large-eye needle, and 2 strips of fabric (1 inch by 22 inches).

To make the garland, wrap and tie one end of the wire securely around the middle of one fabric strip. Thread the other end of the wire through one cinnamon stick, the needle, then thread through one bead, 6 apple slices, 1 bead. Remove the needle from the wire and thread the wire through another cinnamon stick, the needle etc. Repeat using up the remaining beads, apple slices, and cinnamon sticks. Wrap and tie wire around the second strip of fabric. Cut off any excess wire. The garland hangs well on a fireplace or banister.

Saturday September 25

MY grandson Fred has recently taken up golf, and is suffering through the frustrations that come with the game. His golf joke for today left me laughing.

A temperamental golfer hit four balls in succession into a pond. In complete frustration, he threw his bag of clubs into the pond, stomped into the clubhouse, set fire to his clothes, and slashed his wrists. As he was being carried on the stretcher to the ambulance, he spotted his golfing partner. "Hey Mark," he croaked weakly, "what time do we tee off tomorrow?"

Sunday September 26

We plough the fields, and scatter
The good seed on the land,
But it is fed and watered
By God's almighty hand:
He sends the snow in winter,
The warmth to swell the grain,
The breezes, and the sunshine,
And soft refreshing rain.
All good gifts around us
Are sent from heaven above,
Then thank the Lord, O thank the Lord,
For all His love.

Mathew Claudius

Monday September 27

I DO not know what I may appear to the world, but to myself I seem to have been only like a boy playing on a seashore, and diverting myself in the now and then finding a prettier shell, or a smoother pebble than ordinary, whilst the great ocean of truth lay undiscovered before me.

Isaac Newton

Tuesday September 28

WHAT an enormous magnifier is tradition! How a thing grows in the human memory and in the human imagination, when love, worship, and all that lies in the human heart, is there to encourage it.

Thomas Carlyle

Wednesday September 29

OF all God's creatures, there is only one that cannot be made the slave of the leash. That one is the cat. If man could be crossed with the cat, it would improve man, but it would deteriorate the cat.

Mark Twain

Thursday September 30

I SING the praise of the unknown teacher…. He awakens sleeping spirits. He quickens the indolent, encourages the eager, and steadies the unstable. He communicates his own joy in learning and shares with boys and gives the best treasures of his mind. He lights many candles, which in later years, will shine back to cheer him.

Henry van Dyke

October

Friday October 1

Now the autumn trees
    march upon their triumph—
They stand against the faultless
    scrap of blue, blue sky;
Like stained glass windows
    framed with earth's cathedral,
Their colours beg a prayer
    from every passer-by.

Warm depths of holt gold;
    soft gleaming chalices
Bright, intricate, leaf-twined
    and blazened deep with red....
Sunlight filters through the green
    with points of saffron.
The wealth and glory
    of the year exhibited

In one bright flare of beauty
    that so soon must die.
This window, wild with colour,
    is a perfect thing;

And when the night descends
    upon the year, our hearts
Will know its beauty
    and will wear its colouring.

Author unknown

Saturday October 2

FOR several years now, our family has been involved in our local fall fair, and this weekend each of us will enjoy our favourite section of this fine Ontario tradition.

Jenny and Bethany will head for the horse show. For Bruce, Marshall, and Bill, the livestock barns are a source of great interest. Justin and his young cousin Michael are happiest at the "Demolition Derby." Marg, Phyllis, Jamie, and I will spend our time viewing the crafts and displays, or sampling the many homemade foods set out to tempt us.

The Fall Fair is a delightful way to take a look at old and new traditions.

Sunday October 3

For the beauty of the earth,
For the glory of the skies,
For the love which from our birth
Over and around us lies:

Lord of all, to Thee we raise
This our hymn of grateful praise.

For the beauty of human love,
Brother, sister, parent, child,
Friend on earth and friends above,
For all gentle thoughts and mild:
Lord of all, to Thee we raise
This our hymn of grateful praise.

F. S. Pierpoint

Monday October 4

DISSATISFACTION with the world in which we live, and determination to realize one that shall be better, are the prevailing characteristics of the modern spirit.

Goldsworthy Lowes Dickinson

Tuesday October 5

TO know one specific field expertly may give you fame, reputation, and a niche in life. But to know life itself, in all its variety, its goodness and pain, its glory and squalour, you need to know something about many fields.

And, if you care enough, you will know.

Wednesday October 6

THE official baseball records include the names of twelve amateurs who participated in a single major-league game.

This unusual turn of events was precipitated by Tyrus Raymond Cobb. On the afternoon of May 17, 1912, "Ty" took exception to the heckling of a fan in the grandstand, climbed up to where he was seated and socked him in the jaw. For this act, Cobb was fined and suspended—and the whole Detroit Tigers team, in sympathy with their illustrious centre fielder, walked out on strike.

The Athletics management hired amateur "sandlot" players to substitute for the Tigers. Several thousand fans turned out to see what would happen when a big-league ball team played a bunch of rank amateurs. They saw plenty. The Athletics made 26 hits and squeaked out a win over the amateurs—24–2! The strike was settled that night.

Thursday October 7

READING good books is like having a conversation with the highly worthy persons of the past who wrote them; indeed, it is like having prepared conversation in which those persons disclose to us only their best thinking.

René Descartes

Friday October 8

MY friends Will and Muriel took me out to dinner this evening. We went to a small restaurant that specializes in homemade burgers and fries. This restaurant is small, crowded, loud—and they make absolutely wonderful burgers! I laughed when I heard our order for one rare, one medium, and one well-done burger called aloud: "That'll be one cow, walking, one regular, and one hockey puck at table three, please!"

Saturday October 9

HOW quickly the time passes. Today we celebrate the fourth birthday of my youngest great-grandchild, Michael. I can't help but marvel at the way families continue—and I find it comforting to think that some small part of me will be here long after I am gone.

Sunday October 10

ALMIGHTY and everlasting God, who crownest the year with goodness, and hast given unto us the fruits of the earth in her season: Give us grateful hearts, that we may unfeignedly thank Thee for all Thy loving kindness, and worthily magnify Thy holy Name; through Jesus Christ our Lord. Amen.

Monday October 11

Thanksgiving Day

IT is a glorious fall day—a perfect day to enjoy the special family celebration that is a Canadian Thanksgiving.

This year our family has gathered at the country home of my grandson Fred and his wife June. All of us worked together to prepare the meal ahead of time, so that we could take time to walk in the woods and enjoy some family time.

I think this is what Thanksgiving really means to me—quiet time, enjoying the beauty of the season, hours spent in the loving company of family, a delicious meal with the chatter and laughter of little ones adding to the general happy confusion.

Of everything in this world that I am grateful for, I am most thankful for the love of my wonderful family.

Tuesday October 12

MY son-in-law John is a minister. For a number of years, he has collected witty or unusual signs or notices that he has seen on church signboards or in their news publications. Here are just a few of his favourites.

Sign on a church parking lot in Wasaga Beach: "Angel parking only"

After a tornado nearly destroyed a church in Sudbury, this sign was posted: "Praise the Lord, anyway"

This announcement came from the church bulletin board from a tiny village in Essex, England: "Please join us for our Christmas Eve nativity production. A great show—been running for almost two thousand years."

A sign posted outside a church in Toronto read: "Work for the Lord. The pay isn't much, but the retirement benefits are out of this world."

Wednesday October 13

WE forget that the measure of the value of a nation to the world is neither the bushel nor the barrel, but the mind; and that wheat and pork, though useful and necessary, are but dross in comparison with those intellectual products which alone are imperishable.

Sir William Osler

Thursday October 14

> It's autumn in the country now.
> It's autumn in the town.
> October trips with scarlet lips,
> In blue and amber gown!
> The cornfields soon will lie knee-deep
> In snow's white mystery,
> But autumn's in the country now
> Right where I long to be!

Friday October 15

THANK God every morning when you get up that you have something to do that day which must get done, whether you like it or not. Being forced to work, and forced to do your best, will breed in you temperance and self-control, diligence and strength of will, cheerfulness and content, and a hundred virtues which the idle never know.

Charles Kingsley

Saturday October 16

THIS day is a sports fan's dream: baseball, football, and hockey all in the same day! For serious "couch potatoes," snack food will be very important. This recipe for a "Popcorn-Peanut

Munchie" will make you very popular with those family members who will be glued to the television set to "root, root, root for the home team."

3 tbsp. peanut butter
2 tbsp. butter (or margarine)
1/4 tsp. salt
12 cups popped corn (about 1/3 cup kernels)
1 cup salted dry-roasted peanuts

In a small saucepan, heat peanut butter, butter (or margarine), and salt over low heat, stirring until melted. Place popped corn in a large bowl and pour the peanut butter mixture over it. Add peanuts and toss to mix well. Serve within two hours. Makes about 12 cups.

Sunday October 17

O LORD, support us all the day long, until the shadows lengthen and the evening comes, and the busy world is hushed, and the fever of life is over, and our work is done. Then in Thy mercy grant us a safe lodging, and a holy rest, and peace at the last.

Family Prayer at Night

Monday October 18

WHAT is life? It is a flash of a firefly in the night. It is a breath of a buffalo in the winter time. It is as the little shadow that runs across the grass and loses itself in the sunset.

Crowfoot, Blackfoot Chief,
shortly before his death in 1890

Tuesday October 19

THIS is October!
Pumpkins and children glowing from an inner light!

Ange Lewis

Indian summer scalping time from pale-face winter.

Ned Gerber

Ghosts flying every which way.

Jane Hunt Clark

Wednesday October 20

DIFFICULTIES are God's errands; and when we are set upon them, we should esteem it a proof of God's confidence.

Henry Ward Beecher

Thursday October 21

HALLOWEEN has provided an unexpected dividend for two high school students in Skipworth, Virginia.

The two boys were trying to create some gooey slime for use at a Halloween party, and were using the school lab to work on their concoction. When the slime boiled over, it blew up all over the lab.

The disappointed boys cleaned up, but missed a container from another experiment. A small portion of the slime landed in this container and created an incredible new substance which, when sold to one of the many companies lining up to buy it, will make the boys millions of dollars.

The protein-based gelatin slime sticks to paper, stainless steel, and even Teflon, doesn't dissolve in water, but does in saliva, can be eaten like candy, and can be made into a thick sheet that is brittle like glass.

Experts from NASA and DuPont have approached the boys, who have applied for a patent to have their substance protected.

Friday October 22

Life is the childhood of our immortality.

Johann W. von Goethe

Saturday October 23

SOMETIMES we think success is an intrinsic gift with which a person was born. Yet, more often than not, people who have achieved top recognition in their chosen fields have devoted untold years to the development of their talents.

Single-mindedness of purpose and sacrifice are integral parts of most success stories. It doesn't happen overnight, as some might believe.

If you have a talent that you hope to develop, you must decide how much time, energy, and dedication you are willing to give to that end. The quality of your commitment will determine, to a large extent, the quality that results.

The only place where success comes before work is in the dictionary.

Vidal Sassoon

Sunday October 24

FOR what is your life? It is even a vapour, that appeareth for a little time, and then vanisheth away.

James 4:14

Monday October 25

MY son-in-law Bruce flopped down on the couch this evening and sighed, "Who wants to hear about my day?

"The computer system at the office went down five different times today. Every time it malfunctioned, more work accumulated. I decided to stay late and try to catch up, so it was late when I left and I was driving more quickly than I should have been. Suddenly, I heard sirens—a quick look in the rear-view mirror showed the flashing lights of a police car. I pulled over and tried to explain to the officer what a bad day I had been having.

"The officer was very pleasant and listened politely—before heading back to her car to write up the ticket.

"After what seemed like forever, she returned with a big smile on her face.

"'Well sir, your day just got better. Our computers are down and I won't be able to give you a ticket!'

"So, a computer ruined my day and made my day!"

Tuesday October 26

MID-LIFE crisis is that moment when you realize that your children and your clothes are about the same age.

Bill Tammeus

Wednesday October 27

WHEN I was young, I admired clever people. Now that I am old, I admire kind people.

Abraham Joshua Heschel

Thursday October 28

SOME people think only intellect counts: knowing how to solve problems, knowing how to get by, knowing how to identify an advantage and seize it. But the many functions of intellect are insufficient without courage, love, friendship, empathy and compassion.

We care. It is our curse. It is our blessing.

Dean Koontz

Friday October 29

THE true meaning of life is to plant trees, under whose shade you do not expect to sit.

Nelson Henderson

Saturday October 30

WE made a trip today to the "MerryBrook Farm" in Halton, to choose our pumpkins for Halloween. There was a wonderful selection, and we chose a number of the pumpkins in a variety of sizes. As well as a jack-o-lantern, Marg has plans for several other decorations using these colourful squashes, including autumn lanterns for the patio. For these attractive decorations, you cut a lid and scoop out the pulp and seeds. With a pencil or a washable marker, draw a dot pattern on the shell. Using a power screwdriver or a drill with a large bit, drill a hole through each dot. Scrape the inside again and place a candle in each pumpkin.

"Grandpa Bruce" is going to spend his evening carving the jack-o-lantern with his grandchildren.

By tomorrow, we should be ready for our "Ghosts and ghoulies and long-legged beasties!"

Sunday October 31

MY days are swifter than a weaver's shuttle.

Job 7:6

November

Monday November 1

All Saints Day

MOST merciful Father, who hast been pleased to take unto thyself our brethren departed: Grant to us who are still in our pilgrimage, and who walk as yet by faith, that having served thee faithfully in this world, we may, with all faithful Christian souls, be joined hereafter to the company of thy blessed Saints in glory; through Jesus Christ our Lord, who with thee and the Holy Spirit liveth and reigneth, one God, world without end. Amen.

Collect for All Saints Day
Book of Common Prayer

Tuesday November 2

GRANDCHILDREN are a renewal of life, a little bit of us going into the future.

H. S. Barnhart

Wednesday November 3

ON the night of April 14, 1912, the *R.M.S. Titanic*, considered to be unsinkable, struck an iceberg off the coast of Newfoundland and went to the bottom of the Atlantic. Its sinking has been a source of fascination to historians, writers, and movie makers. The Hollywood film *Titanic* won 11 Academy Awards in 1998 and became the biggest box-office movie in history.

It was always thought that the iceberg sliced a gash in the side of the liner, causing the great ship's demise. Recently, another theory has come to light. Tim Foecke, a scientist working at the U. S. National Institute of Standards and Technology, feels that he may have found a fatal flaw in the ship's rivets that caused them to pop. According to Foecke, tests have shown that there was a structural defect in the rivets and when the ship struck the iceberg, they popped, unzipping seams in the hull plates in six places.

Does this mean that the Titanic was poorly built? According to William H. Garzke Jr., a naval architect, "The shipyard bought the best material it could.... There was no reason for it to skimp on materials." It is quite possible that these rivets were the very best available at the time. Apparently they simply were not good enough to prevent a catastrophe.

Thursday November 4

I like to watch the leaves that dance
Upon November trees;
I like to hear the way they laugh
Their answer to the breeze.

I like the gallant gowns they wear,
Of gold and scarlet made,
I even like to watch them fall,
So crisp, so unafraid!

They lend my heart a little prayer,
They give me strength to say:
"When autumn comes into my life,
Let me be brave and gay!

Grant me the grace to laugh and dance
As to the branch I cling,
And let me wear a scarlet gown
And dream of youth and spring!"

Margaret Sangster

Friday November 5

READING is the work of an alert mind, is demanding, and under the ideal conditions produces finally a sort of ecstasy. This gives the experience of reading a sublimity and power unequalled by any other form of communication.

E. B. White

Saturday November 6

A GREAT man is he who has not lost the heart of a child.

Mencius

Sunday November 7

N EITHER do men light a candle and put it under a bushel, but on a candlestick; and it giveth light unto all that are in the house.

Matthew 5:15

Monday November 8

M Y friend Enid made me laugh today with this story in her letter from Calgary.

"You'll remember, Edna, that my grand-daughter Kelly and her husband Jeff are both students in graduate school. They have a very tight budget, so Jeff decided to have Kelly trim his hair. She did her best, but after about an hour of work, Jeff looked like a porcupine.

"Hoping to salvage his appearance (and their savings), Jeff went to the local hairdressing school and took a seat. The student hairdresser greeted him and then disappeared. She returned with her instructor and explained, 'I had to bring my supervisor to make sure she knew you came in looking like this.' Then, turning to her instructor, she said, 'I haven't touched his hair yet—honestly.'

"Jeff got his hair cut and he and Kelly have agreed to look for savings elsewhere."

Tuesday November 9

WE all have unexpected emergencies that demand we graciously feed others at a moment's notice.

My daughter Julia has an excellent plan for just such a contingency. In a kitchen cabinet, Julia has posted a list of dishes that use only pantry and frozen staples. Whenever she uses a menu from the list, she replaces the ingredients that were used.

When life is busy, it's nice to know that company for dinner can be enjoyable for all— even the host and hostess.

Wednesday November 10

I FIND the great thing in this world is not so much where we stand, as in what direction we are moving. To reach the port of heaven, we must sail sometimes against it—but we must sail, and not drift, nor lie at anchor.

Oliver Wendell Holmes

Thursday November 11

Remembrance Day

TODAY a bird sang for me. Today I leaned against the strong trunk of a living tree. Today a little lizard ran across my hand. So I am not alone. When I get back to Canada, I'll remember this. I will cherish all of life, for all life is really one. I will never again be a destroyer, though that is what Man is. This is my dream, that we will learn to live in harmony, not between man alone, but with the whole living world.

> *From a letter found among the effects of a*
> *Canadian infantry soldier killed in Italy,*
> *December 1943*

Friday November 12

GIVE me a few friends who will love me for what I am, or am not, and keep ever burning before my wandering steps, the kindly light of hope. And, though age and infirmity overtake me, and I came not in sight of the castle of my dreams, teach me still to be thankful for life and time's old memories that are good and sweet. And may the evening twilight find me gentle still.

Saturday November 13

THERE is a distinct, if subtle, difference between the cynic and the skeptic. Confronted with something that seems too good to be true, the cynic doubts that it is true, while the skeptic doubts that it is good.

Sydney J. Harris

Sunday November 14

Through all the changing scenes of life,
In troubles and in joy,
The praises of my God shall still
My heart and tongue employ.

To Father, Son and Holy Ghost,
The God whom we adore,
Be glory, as it was, is now,
And shall be evermore.

Tate and Brady

Monday November 15

SEVERAL days ago, I met a gentleman whom I do not see regularly. Once in a while, our paths cross and we reminisce.

I have never seen this man in other than an optimistic mood…always cheerful, always encouraging, always a bright outlook on life. And yet I know that his life has not always been easy. He has had more than his share of ups and downs, yet he retains his optimism and his faith in the goodness of people.

He always greets me with a smile that makes me feel as if I have missed something by not seeing him more frequently.

My friend has a wonderful philosophy of life. It is worth cultivating.

Tuesday November 16

A DEAR family friend called today to tell me that she had become a grandmother. The wonder of becoming a grandparent, and the overwhelming emotion that a newborn grandchild evokes, often takes us by surprise. Those of you who are grandparents will appreciate the thoughts expressed here today.

Going to my grandparents was a highlight of my childhood summers....I was doted upon, admired, entertained, and overfed. I was never more content and happy.

Carolyn Anthony

Soon I will be an old, white-haired lady, into whose lap someone places a baby, saying, "Smile Grandma!"—I who myself so recently was photographed on my grandmother's lap.

Liv Ullmann

The bond between child and grandparent can indeed be the purest, least complicated form of human love.

Foster W. Cline

Wednesday November 17

BEFORE Louis Armstrong became world famous, he would spend a lot of time walking in his neighbourhood on the south edge of Chicago. One afternoon he noticed a small crowd gathered around two street musicians. He stopped to listen, and, to his delight, they were playing an improvised chorus of "Struttin' with Some Barbecue." At the finish of the number, Armstrong walked over and said, "Man, you're playing that too slow!"

"How would you know?" the musicians asked.

"I'm Louis Armstrong, that's my chorus you're playing!"

The next day the pair were back playing at the same spot. This time, there was a sign attached to their tin cup: "Pupils of Louis Armstrong!"

Thursday November 18

IDEALS are like stars; you will not succeed in touching them with your hands. But like the seafaring man on the desert of waters, you choose them as your guides, and following them you will reach your destiny.

Carl Schurz

Friday November 19

ALL would live long, but none would be old.

Benjamin Franklin

Saturday November 20

AS the weather becomes colder and the days are grey and dreary, we often turn to "comfort foods" to cheer us. One of my favourites has always been soup. My friend Mavis sends along her recipe for puréed vegetable soup, a family choice.

1 tbsp. vegetable oil
1 medium onion, chopped
1 clove of garlic, minced
3 green onions
1 bag carrots (16 oz.), sliced
1 small fennel bulb, trimmed and diced
2 cans chicken broth (14 1/2 oz. each)
1/4 tsp. salt
1/4 tsp. black pepper
3 medium potatoes (peeled and quartered)
1/2 cup half and half cream (light)
dill sprigs for garnish

In a 5-quart saucepan, heat oil over medium heat. Add onion, garlic, and green onions and cook 10 minutes or until tender, stirring occasionally. Stir in carrots, fennel, broth, salt, and pepper and 3 cups of water. Heat to boiling over high heat. Reduce heat to low, cover and simmer for 10 minutes. Add potatoes and simmer 20 minutes longer or until the vegetables are very tender. Using a blender on low speed, with the centre part of the cover removed to allow the steam to escape, blend the vegetable mixture, in small batches, until smooth; pour into a large bowl.

Return the mixture to the saucepan; add the half and half cream; heat through. Garnish each serving with a dill sprig. Makes 6–8 servings.

Sunday November 21

ONE of the loveliest prayers is one of the first that we learn.

Our Father who art in heaven,
Hallowed be thy Name, Thy kingdom come,
Thy will be done, on earth as it is in heaven.
Give us this day, our daily bread;
And forgive us our trespasses,
As we forgive those who trespass against us;
And lead us not into temptation,
But deliver us from evil.
For thine is the kingdom, the power, and the glory,
Forever and ever. Amen.

Monday November 22

LILA has made a most difficult decision. She has made arrangements to sell her home and move into a retirement residence. As Lila said, "I feel that this is the right time for me to move, Edna. You know that I haven't been very well for the last few years. My family, friends, and neighbours have been so helpful, and I will be forever grateful for their assistance. But I need more help now than I can ask them to give, and I know that I will receive the best care at the home.

"I'll be sad to leave this old house, but I'm hoping that a young family will buy it and fill it with children's laughter again. I won't be leaving it behind—my memories are going with me."

Tuesday November 23

I HAVE a remarkable memory. I forget everything. It is wonderfully convenient. It is as though the world were constantly renewing itself for me.

Jules Renard

Wednesday November 24

LILA and I had a most enjoyable afternoon together. Although she will be able to choose a few of her favourite possessions to take with her, she needs to decide where she wishes to send the rest. The two of us spent several hours putting names on furniture, artwork, and other treasures that Lila will give pass on when she moves into her retirement residence.

"This silver tea set belonged to my great-grandmother. She brought it with her all the way from England. When she and my great-grandfather first arrived in Canada, they had a log home and very little else, except the silver tea service. They worked hard, and it wasn't long before they had a home worthy of the tea service. It was my great-grandparents' gift to John and me when we were married. I believe I shall give it to Shawna when she and Jason get married in January. You know, most people pass away before their possessions are given away. This is much more fun, I think!"

Thursday November 25

THIS is the day that our friends to the south celebrate Thanksgiving. In homes all across the United States, families are gathering to share in the traditional turkey dinner. I wish each of my American friends a Happy Thanksgiving.

Come, ye thankful people, come,
Raise the song of Harvest-home;
All is safely gathered in,
Ere the winter storms begin.

Henry Alford

Friday November 26

TODAY is the day I have been looking for. All my life has been spent in preparation for it. Yesterday and tomorrow are faraway nothings—the one a faint memory and the other a vague promise. But this is my day. It offers all that God has to give, and I'm a laggard or a coward if I fail to make the most of it.

Saturday November 27

A KIND word is never lost. It keeps going on and on, from one person to another, until at last it comes back to you again.

Sunday November 28

THIS is the first Sunday in Advent, and in church this morning I enjoyed singing this familiar hymn by Charles Wesley.

Come Thou long expected Jesus,
    born to set thy people free:
Free from our fears and sins release us,
    let us find our rest in Thee.
Born Thy people to deliver,
    born a child and yet a king,
Born to reign in us forever,
    now Thy gracious kingdom bring.

Monday November 29

Our minutes are like precious gold
To save or throw away,
They either bring us joy untold
Or sorrow and dismay.
So give to every day its due
In honest, earnest toil,
The harvest pays in measure true
As each man tills his soil.
'Tis he, who ever daily spends
His time in useful ways,
Who reaps rich store of dividends
In happy future days.

Tuesday November 30

WE awoke this morning to a world of white. The first snow of the season always seems to catch us by surprise…one day we see the world in shades of brown and grey, and then the snow falls and we are treated to a day that sparkles and dazzles the eyes.

Oh, this is the glory of winter…
A loveliness unsurpassed,
That follows the haze
Of autumn days
When first snow comes at last.

December

Wednesday December 1

MARG and I received a wonderful surprise this afternoon. Our local florist knocked on the door with a delivery of a dozen poinsettia plants, addressed to, "Two lovely ladies, from a Secret Admirer." I can hardly imagine anyone being so generous, and Marg and I have spent several hours trying to guess who might have shown such kindness to us.

You can't imagine how beautiful our home looks! I know of no better way to decorate than with poinsettia plants. Those that we received today are particularly beautiful—a deep red with just the lightest spray of a gold dust.

Marg has placed several candles near the plants and the gold sparkles in the soft glow of the candlelight.

A kind heart is a fountain of gladness making everything in its vicinity freshen into smiles.

Washington Irving

Thursday December 2

FOR those of us on a fixed income, finding appropriate Christmas gifts that fit the budget can often be quite a challenge. A little ingenuity goes a long way. Friends and readers have offered many suggestions, and today I would like to pass along some of my favourites.

A small basket filled with an assortment of teas, spices, biscuits, and candies is a gift appreciated by people of all ages.

Many people enjoy baking cookies to give, but my friend Mavis has a more creative idea. For her friends who like to bake, Mavis wraps up the ingredients of her favourite cookies and includes her recipe.

I like to give my friends something that I would appreciate receiving. A box of stationery with a book of postage stamps is a particularly welcome gift for my letter-writing friends.

My friend Will enjoys giving cuttings from his favourite plants with some potting soil and a decorative pot.

Friday December 3

THE spirit of self-help is the root of all genuine growth in the individual; and exhibited in the lives of many, it constitutes the true source of national vigour and strength. Help from without is often enfeebling in its effects, but help from within invariably invigorates.

Samuel Smiles

Saturday December 4

IN warmer climes, there is a delightful Christmas custom that has come, originally, from Spain. *Luminarias*, or "little lights of Christmas," decorate driveways, patios, stairways, and rooftops. These simple lantern-type lights were used for centuries, as the symbolic way to light the arrival of the Christ Child on Christmas Eve.

Sunday December 5

O come, O come, Emmanuel,
And ransom captive Israel,
That mourns in lonely exile here
Until the son of God appear.

Rejoice! Rejoice! Emmanuel
Shall come to thee, O Israel.

Old Latin hymn

Monday December 6

MARG and I enjoyed a wonderful day with our young friends from school. Our "reading buddies," along with the school choir, spent the afternoon at our local nursing home.

After the residents had assembled in the lounge, the choir performed several Christmas carols, and then invited everyone to sing along with a number of other songs of the season.

Our young readers then performed, giving a choral reading of the immortal poem by Clement Moore that begins, "'Twas the night before Christmas...."

The children were thrilled by the applause from residents and staff alike. It was a wonderful sense of accomplishment for youngsters who have had such difficulty with reading.

After a party with cookies and hot chocolate, we returned to school with a proud and happy group of children.

Tuesday December 7

I MUST be getting absent-minded. Whenever I complain that things aren't the way they used to be, I always forget to include myself.

George Burns

Wednesday December 8

AMONG the most popular Christmas decorations are pine cones, used in their natural state, or sprayed with colours of green and red or silver and gold.

There is a lovely old German legend that explains the use of pine cones at Christmas.

A poor woman climbed a mountain to pick pine cones for fuel. Under the tree was a small elf who told her to take only the pine cones from under that one tree.

The woman picked up only those cones, and when she arrived home, she found that they had all turned to pure silver. That is why silver cones are popular decorations at this Christmas season.

Thursday December 9

When we hear the Christmas carols
How our hearts with gladness beat—
Whether in the quiet churches,
Or along the busy street.

Friday December 10

LITTLE ones that you know could help out with these delicious "Christmas Light Cookies."

1 cup creamy peanut butter
1/2 cup margarine or butter
1/2 cup packed brown sugar
1 tsp. baking soda
1/2 tsp. vanilla extract
1/4 tsp. salt
1 large egg
1 1/4 cups all-purpose flour
1/4 cup green and red mini M & M's

In a large bowl, with mixer at medium speed, beat the first 7 ingredients until blended, scraping the bowl occasionally with a rubber spatula. Reduce the speed to low, add flour and beat just until combined.

Pre-heat an oven to 350 degrees. Drop dough by heaping tablespoons, about 2 inches apart, on a large, ungreased cookie sheet. Top each cookie with 6–8 M & M's, gently placing them into the dough.

Bake the cookies 15–20 minutes, until lightly browned. With a spatula, transfer the cookies to a wire rack to cool completely. Repeat with remaining dough.

Store cookies in a tightly covered container. Makes about 2 1/2 dozen cookies.

Saturday December 11

It came upon the midnight clear,
That glorious song of old,
From angels bending near the earth,
To touch their harps of gold:
"Peace on the earth, good will to men,"
From heaven's all gracious King.
The world in solemn stillness lay,
To hear the angels sing.

Rev. E. H. Sears

Sunday December 12

IT was "White Gift Sunday" at our church this morning, a time when all parishioners bring gifts of food—tins of fruit, vegetables, juices or boxes of pasta, cereal or rice—wrapped in plain white paper.

All of the gifts donated today will be boxed for delivery to needy families in time for Christmas. "White Gift Sunday" is a lovely way for children to learn of the joy of giving.

"It is more blessed to give than to receive."

Acts 20:25

Monday December 13

O Father, may that holy star
Grow every year more bright,
And send its glorious beams afar
To fill the world with light.

William Cullen Bryant

Tuesday December 14

MY Christmas cards are long since addressed and mailed and now I wait eagerly each day for the arrival of our mailman and the Christmas greetings that he brings from family and friends.

Today, Bruce showed me a Christmas card he received on his computer. Not only was there a traditional-looking card on the screen, but there was also a musical attachment that, with the push of a key, sang, "Hark! The Herald Angels Sing."

I continue to be amazed by what our computers are able to do, and today's greeting card was just another astonishing feat that I am scarcely able to comprehend. Perhaps computer greetings are the beginning of a tradition for the future.

Wednesday December 15

CHRISTMAS is coming, the geese are getting fat....

Thursday December 16

IF every gift is the token of a personal thought, a friendly feeling, an unselfish interest in the joys of others, then the thought, the feeling, the interest may remain long after the gift is forgotten.

Henry van Dyke

Friday December 17

IT is now 96 years since Orville and Wilbur Wright first flew at Kitty Hawk, North Carolina. I wonder what they might have said today, knowing that man has walked on the moon.

Saturday December 18

THE secret of happiness is to make others believe that they are the cause of it.

Sunday December 19

Once in royal David's city
Stood the lowly cattle shed,
Where a mother laid her baby
In a manger for his bed:
Mary was that mother mild
Jesus Christ her little child.

Cecil Frances Alexander

Monday December 20

I BELIEVE that when the soul disappears from this world, it disappears only to become manifest upon another scene in the wondrous drama of eternity.

Edwin Markham

Tuesday December 21

TODAY is the first official day of winter. The shortest day of the year in the northern hemisphere, it means some areas in the far north will have no daylight at all today!

Wednesday December 22

THE Jewish celebration of Hanukkah takes place around the time of the winter solstice and lasts for eight days.

Hanukkah celebrates religious freedom and commemorates the successful rebellion of the Jews against the Syrians in the Maccabean War of 162 BC.

After the victory, the Temple was cleansed, purified and rededicated, and the Menorah, or perpetual lamp, was re-lit. As the story goes, there was only one jar of sacred oil left, but by some miracle this one jar kept the holy lamp burning for eight days.

My friend Rebecca Goldburg and her family celebrate that miracle by lighting candles of the *chanukkiyah*, the special candelabrum that holds eight candles, to commemorate the eight days of Hanukkah. A special prayer is recited during the lighting of the candles, and while the candles burn, it is a time for songs and games and the giving of gifts to the children.

"A lot of our traditions focus on the children," Rebecca says, "and it's a wonderful time to enjoy with our grandchildren."

Thursday December 23

FOR many people, today is a time for last-minute shopping. A large number of my friends from our local nursing home were off to shop with a group of high school "chapterones."

The young people, with help from some of the staff at school, organized the rental of a bus, using funds raised from bake sales and raffles. Each student was paired with a partner from the nursing home, loaded onto the bus—and then they were off for a day of sightseeing, window shopping, and lunch at a lovely restaurant.

Young people are often criticized for their selfishness, so hearing about this wonderful gesture renews my faith in the goodness of teenagers.

Friday December 24

THE candlelight service on Christmas Eve is one of my most loved of the entire year. As we pass through the door, each of us is given a small, lit taper. We enter to the beautiful organ notes of "Silent Night" and, as more and more people arrive, the electric lights are dimmed until only the candles light the church.

What a beautiful way to herald the arrival of God's son, Jesus Christ.

Saturday December 25

Christmas Day

FOR unto us a child is born, unto us a son is given: and the government shall be upon his shoulder; and his name shall be Wonderful, Counsellor, The Mighty God, The Everlasting Father, The Prince of Peace.

Isaiah 9:6

Sunday December 26

O GOD, who makest us glad with the yearly remembrance of the birth of Thy only Son, Jesus Christ: Grant that as we joyfully receive him as our Redeemer, we may with sure confidence behold him when He shall come again to be our Judge; who liveth and reigneth with thee and the Holy Spirit, now and ever. Amen.

Book of Common Prayer

Monday December 27

WHAT a joyful Christmas we had! One of the loveliest gifts that I received was a framed photograph—a rather informal family portrait taken at Thanksgiving.

We all look so relaxed and happy. It doesn't often happen that we are all together as a family, and when that time is caught on film, it is a picture to treasure.

Tuesday December 28

A FRIEND of mine gave me a most interesting gift for Christmas. Somewhere, she found a replica of the Harper's Bazaar magazine from Christmas 1894, which she knew I would enjoy. How right she was! What I find most interesting are the advertisements.

"The finest stationery is so essential to polite correspondence that it is well to purchase that which is recognized as correct…. Insist on 'Whitings' from the Whiting Paper Company of Holyoke, Mass."

"Begin dinner with soup! It refreshes and prepares the stomach for the digestion of heavier food. One pound of Armour's Extract of Beef will make delicious soup for 6 persons daily, for 40 days."

"If decent care and Jaros Hygenic Underwear won't keep you well, then the sanatorium is your proper home."

We've had a wonderful time reading this century-old magazine.

Wednesday December 29

For Mercy has a human heart
Pity a human face,
And Love, the human form divine,
And Peace, the human dress.

William Blake

Thursday December 30

GO to your friend for sympathy; that is natural. Go to your books for comfort, for counsel. But the time will come when no book, no friend, can decide your problem for you; when nothing can save you, but yourself. Begin now to stand alone.

Angela Morgan

Friday December 31

A S the year ends, we look not just to the start of a new year, but to the beginning of a new millennium. This would seem to be a good time to sit back and reflect on all that we have to be grateful for. Health, the love of family, companionship of good friends are just a few things that make my life such a happy one.

O immortal Lord God, who inhabitest eternity, and hast brought Thy servants to the beginning of another year: Pardon, we humbly beseech thee, our transgressions in the past, bless to us this New Year, and graciously abide with us all the days of our lives; through Jesus Christ our Lord. Amen.